the ultimate guide to

Competency
Assessment

in health care

third edition

by Donna Wright

The Ultimate Guide to Competency Assessment In Health Care, Third Edition
Copyright © 2005 by Donna Wright

Cover design: Jaana Bykonich
Cover artwork: Donna Wright

ISBN 13: 978-1-886624-20-7

Twelfth Printing: June 2016

20 19 18 17 16   16 15 14 13 12

For permission and ordering information, write to:

CREATIVE
HEALTH CARE
MANAGEMENT

Creative Health Care Management, Inc.
5610 Rowland Road, Suite 100
Minneapolis, MN 55343
chcm@chcm.com
800.728.7766 / 952.854.9015
www.chcm.com

To three people who have provided me with their unconditional support:

My parents, Richard & Ramona Kellogg, for their lifelong encouragement to be the best I could be;

And my husband, Jacques Dupret, whose honesty and support refresh my soul everyday.

table of Contents

Chapter Three

Chapter Four

Chapter Five

Chapter Six

Acknowledgements

Everyone knows that projects, like writing a book, do not happen through the energy and talents of just one person. I am very fortunate to have the opportunity to work with many competent and talented people. These people inspire me, challenge me, create with me, and even hold me accountable on occasion. All of these aspects create a competent, creative team. I would like to acknowledge this creative team and thank them for their dedication to this project.

Beth Beaty	Managing Editor
Chris Bjork	Resources Division Director
Rebecca Smith	Editor
Veronica Beaty	Data Entry Specialist
Phillip Schwartzkopf	Marketing Director
Claire Stokes	Indexer
Mori Studio, Inc.	Book design & layout

And the staff and faculty at
Creative Health Care Management.

Thank you. It is a joy to work with such a truly functional team.

Donna Wright

Introduction

It is easy for us to fall into the common competency assessment traps. We can commit to assessing so many competencies that we begin to drown in them. We can get stuck in the trap of measuring the same competencies year after year. And we can become so focused on assessing competencies for the appeasement of outside groups that we inadvertently overlook the competencies that are most essential for our clients' safety and well being.

This book offers an effective, efficient, and meaningful approach to competency assessment—one that really focuses on why competency assessment is important. We do not assess competency for the sake of outside regulatory agencies like Joint Commission, OSHA, and other state and federal agencies. We do competency assessment to assure that we are giving the best possible care to our patients, residents, and other customers—and at the same time shine in our surveys from outside agencies.

This new approach may require us to "stretch" a bit. It may take some courage to not get caught in the old ruts of competency assessment. Competency assessment is not about completing a bunch of competency checklists. If your competency assessment process is loaded with checklists, you are probably measuring many things that focus only on technical skills, and you are likely missing the assessment of critical thinking and interpersonal skills.

Having the courage to look at our processes in a thoughtful, critical manner is essential to the success of competency assessment. Rather than trying to create huge, comprehensive list of skills required for each job and then trying to check them off each year, I suggest we focus on the elements that truly relate to competency assessment success. Close adherence to the six aspects of meaningful competency assessment listed below, will assure that competency assessment works for us, our employees, and our clients. They are:

1. Selecting competencies that matter.

2. Selecting the right verification methods for each competency identified.

3. Clarifying accountability of the manager, educator, and employee in the competency process.

4. Utilizing an employee-centered verification process (where the employee has choices from a selection of verification methods).

5. Identifying what is a competency problem and what is not.

6. Promptly and effectively addressing competency deficits and employee problems once they are identified.

Creating a competency process that has all of these six aspects is easier than you might imagine. It just takes a shift in thinking. With the plan put forth in this book, your competencies lists will be smaller and more meaningful. You'll see that you can assess many skills in daily work, and you'll even learn how you can use competency assessment to motivate, recognize, and create accountability in all employees up and down the organizational ladder.

Even leaving out one of the six aspects can greatly impair our ability to move forward with strong, safe, effective health care services. For example, if we put everything in place to assess competency, but never follow through with problematic employees, we will eventually create an environment that sends the message, "Don't bother to comply; they never do anything about it if you don't!" This attitude will quickly spread throughout the team and eventually the organization.

Competency assessment, by its very nature, shapes the environment in which it is used. This environment can become functional or dysfunctional, depending on how the assessment process is implemented and perceived. If your competency assessment process is inefficient, and therefore perceived as an ineffective, redundant waste of time, it will serve to create a more dysfunctional environment. If competency assessment is meaningful, it will be perceived as a tool that helps to ensure efficient, effective care, and will make the environment in which it exists more functional.

Here is Donna Wright's Competency Assessment Model:

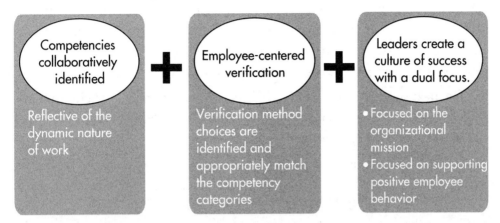

Traditional Competency Assessment vs. Wright's Competency Assessment Model

Traditional Competency Assessment	Wright's Outcome-focused/Account-ability-based Approach
Competencies are determined by leaders (managers, educators, etc.). (Often called "core competencies")	Competencies are identified through a collaborative effort between managers and staff. (Competencies identified in this approach are based on "prioritized need.")
⬇	⬇
Competency verification is done by only a few methods. The two most commonly selected verification methods: • Checklists ("I observe you doing this.") • Tests (Often online test packages)	Competency verification is done through 11 different categories of verification methods. These methods include: • Guided, reflective practice approaches • Outcome measurements of daily work • Verification methods that can actually develop critical thinking skills
Process-focused Approach	**Outcome-focused and Accountability-based Approach**

This outcome focused, accountability based approach to competency assessment may sound like *more* work, but it isn't. Rather that more work, it offers a new way to think about competencies and how to assess them. With reflection on your current systems and a few new tools, the shift to this approach to competency assessment may be easier than you think.

The next six chapters will bring the elements of this model to light. In them, we will explore strategies and examples to put these elements into daily work and support overall organizational goals.

You will find a variety of forms and examples throughout the book. We encourage you to use them to get ideas to enhance your competency program. But keep in mind: IT IS NOT ABOUT THE FORMS! The magic of this process lies in the way you go about identifying competencies and carrying out the assessment process. This is your guide to creating a truly successful competency process. It is a guide that will help you reach your goals and create a truly healthy work environment.

chapter one

The Goal of Competency Assessment

- Goal of competency assessment

- Incorporating regulatory standards

- Defining competency

The Goal of Competency Assessment

Organizations engage in competency assessment in order to:

- evaluate individual performance
- evaluate group performance
- meet standards set by a regulatory agency (Joint Commission, OSHA[1], etc.)
- address problematic issues within the organization
- enhance or replace performance review

No matter what has led your organization to competency assessment, review the intent behind these motivating factors and define why your organization will support and carry out the process of competency assessment.

The assessments themselves can take many forms and address multiple needs for your organization. It is counterproductive to lock your organization into one or two methods of assessment, such as checklists or observer reviews. This book will help you to see your organization's competency assessment process more clearly, while offering a variety of methods for verifying identified competencies.

Competency assessment is a fluid, ongoing process. It helps identify and evaluate the skills necessary to carry out the job *now*, as well as *in the future*, as the job evolves over time. Competency assessment is only meaningful when it reflects the dynamic nature of the job. This means you will not have one list of competencies or skills identified for a job that you will simply check off over and over each year; instead your competencies will be a collection of skills, abilities, and behaviors that address the changing nature of the job for a given period of time. These competencies will only be used for an identified assessment period.

Competency assessment can help groups focus on the philosophy and mission of an organization. Competency assessment can also direct employee participation in—and understanding of—the identified organizational goals for a given period, as well as help each employee understand and verify his or her personal contributions to achieving your organizational goals.

Organizational Evolution and Employee Alignment

Every organization evolves over time to meet the changing needs and demands of the health care environment. Competency assessment identifies the specific skills required in each job class to make your organizational evolution successful. It is prudent to clarify with all employees that their jobs will evolve over time as

---

[1] Occupational Safety and Health Administration

the organization's needs change. No one's job stays the same. Through the competency assessment process, the organization identifies this evolution and invites the employee to evolve with it.

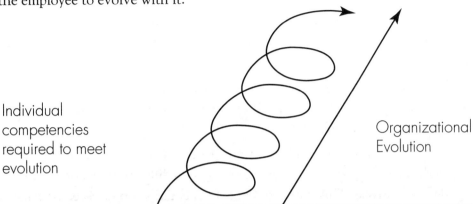

Individual competencies required to meet evolution

Organizational Evolution

In reality, an organization should not evolve to meet an individual employee's needs; instead individuals are invited to grow and evolve with the organization. The organization must help and support its evolution through providing education, time, and resources, so the employee can achieve the new skills necessary to make this evolution successful. The organization must also recognize that if at any time the employee is not comfortable with the organization's direction, the employee can choose to dissolve his or her contractual agreement with the organization. In other words, employees should periodically reflect on their commitment to their organization's evolution, and if that commitment is not strong, find an organization to work for that is better aligned with his or her personal philosophies and goals.

To maintain a successful organization/employee relationship, the employee's evolution must be aligned with the organization's evolution. If at any time the employee goes off in a different direction,

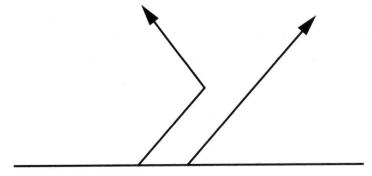

the organization (usually a supervisor or a manager) must discuss this with the employee and tell him or her that he or she must come back in line with the organizational direction. If the employee refuses to come back into alignment, the organization must consider breaking its contractual agreement with the employee. Employees working counter to the organization's philosophy can often sabotage (deliberately or not) the organization's daily operations, and *bending* the organizational philosophy to meet their individual needs is potentially even more dangerous.

I am not saying we should not be supportive to employees. I am saying we need to clearly articulate what direction we are organizationally going and support employees to move in the same direction.

In addition, when an employee begins to divert from this parallel relationship with the organizational evolution, and go in a different direction, this is *not* an educational issue. This is a management issue. Please do not spend a dime of educational money on this issue. I say this because often we do. We send these employees to customer service training or attitude adjustment classes.

The focus of this issue is around organizational commitment. In this situation, the manager needs to ask a basic question related to commitment: "Do you really want to work here?" It is a simple question that is not always easy to ask. So even though this is not an educational or competency issue with the employee, there may be an educational or competency need for the manager. Most of our managers in health care struggle with these tough issues. Most of our managers in health care were promoted to these positions because of their excellent service or clinical skills. Their management competencies may be inadequate. Our organizational support should be directed toward helping the manager discuss this commitment question with the employee when needed, not on remedial education for the employee.

By keeping this concept of organizational evolution in our daily organizational planning, the process of competency assessment can help groups focus on the philosophy and mission of an organization. Competency assessment can also direct employees' participation in and understanding of the identified organizational goals for a given period, as well as help each employee understand and verify his or her contributions to achieving your organizational goals.

Regulatory Standards

Many external regulatory groups dictate the changes we make in our organizations. These groups include The Joint Commission, the Occupational Safety and

Health Administration (OSHA), federal and state regulatory agencies, licensure and certification boards, specialty associations, and so on.

When planning how to incorporate these standards into your daily operation, consider the intent behind each standard. It is always a good idea to read any regulatory standard for yourself, rather than having someone else summarize or interpret it for you. Too often the meaning of the standards seems to change as one individual passes on his or her interpretation of the standard to the next person.

Understanding the Intent Behind Competency Related Standards

Most standards relating to competency assessment, staff development or human resources fall under one of two categories: *providing information* or *measuring competency*.

When you read competency related standards, ask yourself, "Is the intent behind the standard to provide information or to measure competency?"

Providing information:

Providing information standards are those that ask us to give people information or make information accessible or easily retrievable. For example, many state and federal laws require us to inform employees if their benefits packages change. Many OSHA standards direct us to provide employees with information regarding hazardous materials, so that the employee is informed of the nature of his or her job and the daily duties. Response to this type of standard may include education, reference material, or mechanisms for getting information from experts if the employee has questions about the nature of the work or substances/equipment used to carry out the work.

The focus of these standards is on providing pertinent information to employees. Strategies to comply with these standards may include things like providing Material Safety Data Sheet manuals, placing safety or emergency posters in prep areas, or writing memos to individual employees.

Measuring competency:

Many standards, such as the Joint Commission standards, require measurement of competence. Measuring competency focuses on the *verification* or *demonstration* of knowledge, skill, behavior or attitude.

The verification can take many forms and should be appropriate for the organization's competency definition. Education may be part of the competency process to help the individual achieve the desired competency outcome. Education, in and of itself, is not a measure of competency. In other words, just attending an in-service or class does not measure competency, unless a competency verification method is incorporated into the class (i.e., case study, return demo, and so on). So verification is the focus of competency assessment; education is not. Education can help some people reach the goal of verification, but it is not required for everyone. Demonstrating or verifying you *have* the knowledge, skill or ability is the focus.

External and Internal Standards

Besides understanding whether a standard is "providing information" or "measuring competency," it is important to ask whether a standard has come to you from an external source or an internal source. An external standard or policy comes from an external agency, like Joint Commission or OSHA or a federal or state agency. An internal standard comes from your own organization.

It is very important to know the source of the standards your organization follows.

Many people think that some of their standards are from external sources when they are really from their own organizational policies. And many times organizations may be cited by an external agency for a deficit based on what was written in an *internal* policy, not an external policy.

Example:

An external agency states in their standards:
> You must have a fire safety preparedness plan in your organization. The plan should include equipment checks, drills, mock events, and education/training.

An internal policy that someone in your organization writes to reflect the standard above:
> All of our employees will attend our annual fire safety training class every year.

If only 98% of your staff attend the class, you could be cited for a deficiency based on the internal policy your organization wrote, not on the one from the external group.

An external agency can cite an organization for noncompliance with the organization's own internal policy. So read and review your own policies carefully. You will be held accountable to follow what you write.

Competency Defined

Defining competency is essential to establishing a sound competency assessment process.

Each organization should write its own definition of competency. Here are a few that may help you get started:

- The knowledge, skills, abilities, and behaviors needed to carry out a job.
- Whatever is required to do something adequately. (Pollock, 1981).
- The ability to perform a task with desirable outcomes under the varied circumstances of the real world. (Benner, 1982).
- The effective application of knowledge and skill in the work setting. (del Bueno, 1990).

Keep in mind: If your organization's definition of competency requires measurement in real world situations, your competency verification methods should reflect real world situations as well.

Your organization should also construct a policy to help guide your competency assessment process. Effective competency assessment policies will include:

- the definition of what constitutes competency in your organization
- an explanation of the process to be used for assessment
- clarification of the responsibilities of managers, leaders, educators, and staff in the competency assessment process
- clarification of the resources available

Here is a sample of a competency assessment policy:

Organization-Wide Competency Assessment Policy/Procedure

PURPOSE OF COMPETENCY ASSESSMENT

- To provide a mechanism for directing and evaluating the competencies needed by our employees to provide quality health care services to our customers.
- To identify areas of growth and development, and provide opportunities for ongoing learning to achieve continuous quality improvement.

DEFINITION OF COMPETENCY:

Competency is the application of knowledge, skills, and behaviors that are needed to fulfill organizational, departmental, and work setting requirements under the varied circumstances of the real world.

COMPETENCY ASSESSMENT PROCESS:

Competency assessment will occur on an ongoing basis. Competencies will be identified on an annual basis through a collaborative process, and assessed on a continuum throughout the employment of an individual. This continuum will include assessment during the hire process, initial competencies during the orientation period, and ongoing annual competency assessment.

Hire assessment will include validation of...

- Licensure, registration, and certification (where applicable)
- Previous experience and current skills and abilities through the interview process, reference checking, resumes, and applications

Initial competency assessment will include validation of...

- Core job functions
- Frequently used functions and accountabilities
- High risk job functions and accountabilities
- Age specific concepts for customers served

Ongoing competency assessment will include validation of..

- New policies, procedures, technologies, and initiatives
- Changing policies, procedures, technologies, and initiatives
- High risk functions and accountabilities
- Problematic job aspects identified (through quality improvement (QI), incident reports, customer surveys, review of aggregate competency data, etc.)

COMPETENCY ACCOUNTABILITIES DEFINED:

The accountability for competency assessment will occur at three levels: 1) the organizational steering committee for competency assessment, 2) the designated supervisor for each area, and 3) the employee.

The Steering Committee is responsible for...

- Developing a competency definition
- Developing a system for competency documentation
- Providing education and consultation on competency assessment
- Developing organizational competencies
- Developing guidelines and policies for competency assessment
- Developing mechanisms for reporting to governing body
- Evaluating competency program

The manager in each area is responsible for...

- Receiving and distributing information from the steering group
- Establishing a mechanism to identify specific area competencies with staff involvement
- Creating an environment that promotes timely competency assessment and ongoing growth and development
- Providing education to employees on the competency process
- Monitoring employee progress
- Participating in evaluation of the competency process

The employee is responsible for...

- Completing competencies as indicated
- Participating in competency development
- Participating in evaluation of the competency process

Educators/Staff development specialist will provide...

- Expertise to support the steering committee, managers and employees in their areas of responsibility in the competency assessment process.
- Expertise on matching the appropriate verification methods to the competencies identified by the groups indicated above.

Note: The educator's role is *not* to identify the competency for a group or to check off every employee's competencies. The educator will *support* or help *facilitate* the manager and staff in the identification of the competencies, and can help oversee and support competency verification When a group develops and takes ownership of its own program, staff buy-in is greater, and the results are always more successful.

Verification of Individual Competencies:

Each employee will be responsible for completing his or her own competencies using verification methods they select from an approved list for each competency. The manager's role is to validate at the end of the competency period that the employee has successfully completed this process. The employee will be deemed "competent" with the completion of 100% of the indicated competencies for that job class. If successful completion has not been achieved, the employee is "not yet deemed competent," and an action plan is initiated.

Resources available for successful competency assessment

Information regarding competency development, verification methods, educational support, and competency documentation is available from the following departments or in the following documents (insert information for Education Department, Human Resources etc. here):

Definition of Competency Assessment from Joint Commission

The Joint Commission defines competency in a very broad, general way, giving individual organizations a lot of room to define competency in their own way.

Definition of Competency Assessment from Joint Commission

"Capacity equals requirement."

Staff
Abilities
=
Organizational
Goals/Objectives

In a nutshell: Competency assessment should assess, on an ongoing basis, that you have the right staff abilities to carry out your current organizational goals and objectives.

IMPORTANT

Competency assessment, and performance improvement in general, will require ongoing assessment and priority setting. The Joint Commission performance improvement standards encourage ongoing organizational evaluation and monitoring, and expect that priority setting will be part of that process. We will never be able to address all areas for improvement, but we can select those areas that are of highest concern and have the greatest impact on the services we render to our clients.

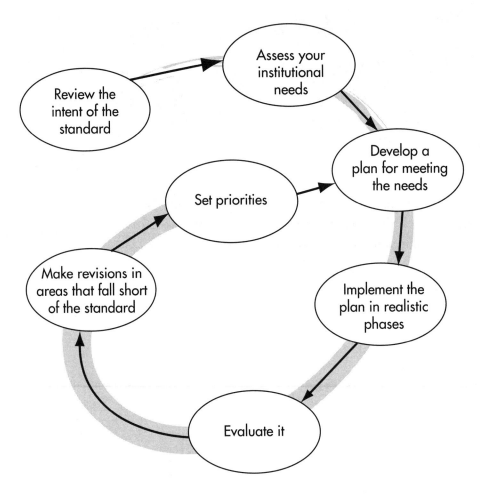

Competency Assessment Is a Dynamic Process

Competency assessment is a fluid, ongoing process. It is dynamic and responsive to the changing environment. Competency assessment should reflect the current direction and demands of your organization's ever-changing environment. It is like sailing; in order to move in a desired direction, we must be able to periodically adjust our sail.

Competency assessment is not a static process that assesses and re-assesses checklists of identified competencies that we check off each year. Organizations using systems that merely check and re-check the same list of competencies year after year find their own competency assessment process frustrating and meaningless. It can become an overwhelming paper chase. These organizations may end up feeling that they are assessing competencies that do not even reflect the current nature of the job classes, and that their competencies frequently need to be revised.

Since our organizations are moving toward a dynamic goal, running around in a circle will not help us to reach the goal.

Why not use a dynamic approach to identifying competencies rather than a static approach? The following chapters will discuss all the elements of creating this dynamic approach to competency assessment/process.

Notes

chapter two

The Essential Elements of Competency Assessment

- Assessing all three domains of competency assessment

- Defining the competency continuum

- Developing initial and ongoing competencies

- Creating meaningful competency assessment

Assessing All Domains of Skill

Individual job skills will vary from job class to job class. However, these three domains are always present whether you are delivering patient care, tending to the custodial needs of the environment, or providing leadership to the organization.

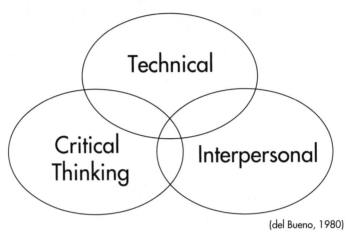

(del Bueno, 1980)

The following are some basic categories within each of the three domains:

Clinical/Technical Skills	Critical Thinking Skills	Interpersonal Skills
• Cognitive skills • Knowledge • Psychomotor skills • Technical understanding (ability to follow directions and carry out procedures)	• Problem solving • Time management • Priority setting • Planning • Creativity • Ethics • Resource allocating • Fiscal responsibilities • Clinical reasoning • Reflective practice • Learning • Change management	• Communication • Customer service • Conflict management • Delegation • Facilitation • Collaboration • Directing others • Articulation • Understanding diversity • Building and nurturing team skills • Listening • Respecting • Caring

Competency Assessment Is an Ongoing Process

Employee skills are assessed in three distinct phases, and are based on the requirements of the job and the ongoing needs of the organization.

Competency Continuum

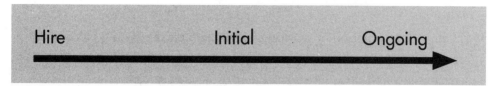

| Hire | Initial | Ongoing |

Competencies are assessed when an individual is hired, during his or her orientation period, and throughout employment as the requirements of the job and the needs of the organization change. Competencies should address the unique needs of each of these periods. You will not have one unchanging list of competencies for a job that you check and re-check during each of these periods. Instead, you will have meaningfully evolving lists of competencies that address each period separately.

Hire

Competency assessment starts before we hire. During the hiring phase, we begin assessing competency through verification of licensure, registration, and certification. We then assess knowledge through one-to-one interviews often using new-hire checklists to assess specific knowledge, skills, and previous experience. We may contact previous employers to verify employment history.

During this period, make sure copies of licensure, registration, certification or other similar evidence is put into the employee file.

Initial Competencies

Initial Competencies focus on the knowledge, skills, and abilities required in the first 6 months to a year of employment (the typical time required for orientation and observation prior to independently carrying out job functions). This is sometimes referred to as the probation period. The initial competency period starts when you hire the person and continues until they are ready to work independently (or post-probation).

Three things will occur during the initial competency period:

1. There will be a period of **centralized orientation.** This is the time spent, usually with centralized educators, staff development people, or human resources specialists, to become oriented to the organizational systems, mission, policies, etc.

2. There will be a period of **decentralized orientation.** This is the time spent with a preceptor, mentor, or buddy to learn the specifics of the job. It is usually done with someone in the same or similar job category.

3. There will be a period of **working independently, but being closely supervised.** This occurs after you are done with orientation. You begin to take assignments and do work independently, but you are closely supervised. A preceptor, charge nurse, team leader, or shift supervisor may check in on you periodically, and be available to answer questions as you start working independently. The supervision at this time is at a much greater frequency and intensity than the supervision of more experienced employees who are working in the same job category.

Ongoing Competencies

Ongoing competency assessment should be done periodically. Many organizations conduct this assessment on an annual basis. The frequency can be defined in your competency-related policies. Joint Commission standards indicate that it should be conducted every three years at minimum.

> Joint Commission Standard HR.3.10: "Competence to perform job responsibilities is assesses, demonstrated, and maintained."

> Element of Performance number 5: "A defined time frame for how often competency assessments are performed for each person, minimally, once in the three-year accreditation cycle and in accordance with law and regulation." (The Joint Commission, 2004)

The ongoing competencies should *build* on the competencies assessed in the hire and initial phases. Your ongoing competencies should *not* be a repeat of the initial competencies or a static list of skills that are checked off again and again each year.

Ongoing competencies should reflect the current nature of the work expected to be carried out by the employees in a job category. These competencies should reflect the new, changing, high risk, and problematic aspects of the job.

Keep these things in mind when developing ongoing competencies for each job class:

- Ongoing competency assessment is a dynamic process that is based on the ever-changing needs required to carry out the organization's mission and goals.
- Ongoing competencies will be different from the initial competencies identified for the job, and will change each competency assessment period.
- Ongoing competency assessment is *not* an annual reassessment of the initial competencies for the job.

Initial Competencies versus Ongoing Competencies

Initial competencies are a collection of skills, knowledge, behaviors and attitudes needed to get started in a new position. Initial competencies will not be used to re-assess in the ongoing competency assessment period. By using the initial competencies over and over again, you act as if the competencies for any job are static, which in the current reality of health care is not true.

In addition, by repeating competencies, year after year, you build your assessment process on the philosophy or assumption that "people lose skills." In reality, employees rarely lose skills. More often, the environment or conditions change in relation to existing skills, so employees need to adapt and advance their skills to accommodate the new conditions.

Some people may argue that people *do* "lose skill." They say after several months, if you have not used the skill, you may not be able to perform. I agree, but I believe you did not "lose" the skill—you are just no longer proficient.

Example:

Many of you know how to ride a bicycle. If I brought a bike to your organization today, I bet you could ride it. Even if it had been 20 or 30 years since you had ridden a bike. Now, I am not saying you would look good riding the bike. You may look awkward and a bit unbalanced, but you could still ride it. You did not lose bike riding skill but you may not be proficient.

Checking people off every year for the same skills sends a message that you might lose skill—which you do not. And furthermore, doing the repeat checks does not really address the proficiency issues that may arise.

From a resource management perspective, it's important to note also that assessment and re-assessment can be very costly. We could check all sorts of skills needed in the organization, but we'd be wise to look specifically at which skills make a real difference in our service delivery, and which skills have significantly changed or need to change. Where do we draw the line? Focusing competency efforts on what makes a difference is the key to quality, cost-effective competency assessment.

Tying competency assessment to quality improvement (QI) or performance improvement (PI) activities can help your organization identify the ongoing skills needed to meet the ever-changing aspects of the health care environment. Tying competency assessment to QI/PI can help you keep the process meaningful and manageable, as it can prevent you from creating a system so monstrous that it becomes ineffective. It can also help you ensure that necessary skills and issues are not missed. This type of approach to competency assessment can help create a system that is more focused on outcomes rather than the process itself. And outcomes are really what matter to our customers.

Competency Development

Initial competencies reflect the knowledge, skills, and behaviors required in the first six months to a year in a particular job class. These are the competencies needed to get started in the job category. They are usually defined by the indicated probation period of the job.

Develop initial competencies based on:

- Core job functions
- Frequently used job functions and accountabilities
- High-risk[1] job functions and accountabilities
- The intended "essence" of the job

Ongoing competencies reflect the ever-changing nature of the job, organization, and environment. As the job, organization, and environment change, so will the competencies necessary to meet the new demands. Ongoing competency assessment is done periodically throughout employment. The frequency of the assessment is determined by the organization.

---

[1] High-risk refers to anything that would cause harm or death to customers, or result in legal action against employees or the organization.

Develop ongoing competencies based on:

- New initiatives, procedures, technologies, policies, practices, patient/ customer populations, etc.
- Changes in procedures, technologies, policies, practices, patient/ customer populations, etc.
- High-risk job functions and accountabilities
- Problematic areas identified by QI/PI data, patient surveys, staff surveys, incident reports, or any other formal or informal evaluation processes

Initial Competency Development

The initial competencies focus on the job skills and abilities needed in the first six months to a year of a new job. These are the competencies that get a new employee started in the job. The goal of the initial competencies is *not* to assess every skill ever needed in the job, but to assess the skills needed during the introductory or probationary period. When developing initial competencies, ask yourself, "What do I want this employee to be able to do at the end of the probationary period?" This will be just the basics to get them safely started in the job.

Initial competencies go beyond orientation. They reflect the performance of the new employee in centralized orientation, decentralized orientation (preceptoring time), and a period where the employee starts to work independently, but is under close supervision. The purpose of initial competency assessment is to answer the basic question: "Should this person pass probation?"

Most people, when creating initial competencies, create 17 to 20 pages of checklists of different skills. These skills are then checked off by a variety of orientation coordinators and preceptors. These lists can be overwhelming and confusing to a new employee and often tend to only reflect technical aspects of the job. When orientation is complete and the new employee starts working independently, coworkers report that the new employee still does not *really* "get the job."

There is a better approach to initial competency assessment. Don't throw away the 17 to 20 pages of checklists; they have a purpose. Let them act as a guide to remind the preceptor(s) what to show the new person.

When creating initial competencies, try to capture the "essence of the job." This can be done in as few as 5 to 7 basic competency statements. These statements should capture the overall outcome goals of the job. They should include the attitudes and understandings of the job that help an employee to be truly successful.

Example:

Here are some initial competency statements that capture the "essence of the job" for the position of Intensive Care Unit (ICU) nurse:

- *Ability to monitor (monitoring the patient's condition, monitoring machines, monitoring family dynamics, monitoring team dynamics)*
- *Ability to communicate concisely (verbally and written charting and documentation)*
- *Ability to "have a little attitude" (have enough confidence to assertively assess patient and team concerns—we all know what ICU attitude looks like. We need it. When appropriately used it can save a patient's life!)*
- *Ability to "learn on the fly." (can look things up, initiate their own education, not afraid to state their areas of uncertainty and do something about it.)*
- *Ability to respond in emergencies (includes not just the demonstration of BLS—Basic Life Support and ACLS—Advanced Cardiac Life Support but also the ability to respond in an emergency in a real or mock event.)*

These five statements capture the basic essence of an ICU nurse job. It is not pages of checklists with multiple tasks to check off, but instead describes the "essence of the job." It gives the new employees a better understanding of the overall job goals.

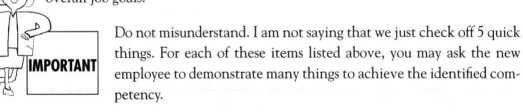

Do not misunderstand. I am not saying that we just check off 5 quick things. For each of these items listed above, you may ask the new employee to demonstrate many things to achieve the identified competency.

For example:

To demonstrate the "monitoring" competency, you may ask the employee to demonstrate monitoring several different pieces of equipment and present a case presentation where they discuss how they picked up on subtle changes in their patient's condition and monitored family dynamics. All this is just to demonstrate the "monitoring" competency.

But overall, these basic initial competency statements give a wonderful picture of the essence of the job to the new employee.

Ongoing Competency Development

Since every organization is constantly growing and evolving, our jobs need to reflect this ever-changing dynamic reality. Ongoing competencies are not a static list of skills that never change. Ongoing competencies need to reflect the ever-changing nature of the job in light of both the ever-changing nature of the job and the organization's missions and goals.

When developing ongoing competencies, start by assessing the changing nature of the environment. Do not start by merely identifying the important aspects of the job. Although these aspects are **IMPORTANT** essential to the job, they do not necessarily need to be re-assessed after the initial competency assessment, unless they are also identified as a changing or problematic part of the job.

We must then identify a way to focus on the competencies needed at any point during our organization's evolution. The Worksheet for Identifying Ongoing Competencies (page 25) can be used to identify the competencies needed for each job for a given period. Brainstorm competency issues for each of the four categories listed on the worksheet. Then prioritize the issues identified. *The competencies selected should be those skills needed by 100% of employees in the job class.* This is not a list of educational in-service needs; it is a representation of the minimal changing skills needed by everyone in the job category to carry out the current job.

To make the ongoing competencies meaningful and achievable, select 10 or fewer competencies to focus on for each given assessment period. Organizations are not required to check off every skill needed to carry out a job every year. Instead, focus on the competencies for each job class that most affect your organization's services and outcomes.

Some groups select too many competencies for a given period. It can be difficult for the employee to accomplish the verification of a large list of competencies in a meaningful way. In these situations, some organizations have started out with large lists of competencies and were unable to complete them. So a secondary, condensed version of the competencies is often substituted half way through the year. This approach creates bitter feelings about the competency process for both staff and managers. It also undermines the overall credibility of the competency assessment process and outcomes.

When developing your competency list for each job class, keep it achievable. I recommend 10 or fewer competencies over whatever time period you select.

Use the ongoing competency worksheet to prioritize the competencies you have identified.

Early success in the competency assessment process will create acceptance and employee buy-in to the process. When the competency process is viewed as meaningful by the employees and helps guide them in achieving the organization's goals for the year, it will help build more collaboration among our teams and departments.

Preparing to Complete the Worksheet for Identifying Ongoing Competency

In order to successfully identify your true ongoing competency needs, you need to have the right people around the table when completing this worksheet. Minimally you need people from two categories around the decision-making table: 1) the **manager** for the job category, and 2) some **employees** currently working in the job category. The manager's input is necessary because he or she is ultimately responsible for the service provided in that area. Employee input is necessary because employees do the job every day.

The decision-making table can be rounded out by educators, staff development specialists, human resources personnel, clinical nurse specialists, quality improvement coordinators, and other support people. Remember, however, that these support people cannot do it *for* the manager and staff without their involvement.

As you fill out the Worksheet for Identifying Ongoing Competencies you should have the following documents in front of you. They will help guide your group to consider the most important aspects of the job.

- ❑ Job description
- ❑ Organization mission statement
- ❑ Some of the Joint Commission screening indicators (QI data, patient satisfaction surveys, etc.)
- ❑ Scope of practice/service documents
- ❑ Any other organizational/departmental vision statements

Worksheet for Identifying Ongoing Competencies

Job Class   _____

Dept./Area   _____

Date   _____

Step 1: Brainstorm staff needs in each of the categories listed below.

Step 2: Prioritize those needs and choose which ones the organization will focus on. (see page 27 for prioritization guidelines.)

Competency Needs:	Priority: Hi-Med-Lo
What are the NEW procedures, policies, equipment, initiatives, etc. that affect this job class	
What are the CHANGES in procedures, polices, equipment, initiative, etc. that affect this job class.	

© Creative Health Care Management • www.chcm.com • 800.728.7766

Competency Needs:	Priority: Hi-Med-Lo
What are the HIGH RISK aspects of this job. (High risk is anything that would cause harm, death or legal action to an individual or the organization.)	
What are the PROBLEMATIC aspects of this job. (These can be identified through quality management data, incident reports, patient surveys, staff surveys, and any other form of formal or informal evaluation.)	

Try to limit your focus to 10 or fewer competencies each year. Trying to focus on more than that can be confusing and overwhelming for both staff and leaders.

Reminder:

Are there any age-specific[1] aspects in any of the priority areas listed above? Add age-specific aspects to a competency selected above, rather than creating a separate age-specific competency (see chapter 5).

[1]You can also consider cultural and other population-specific aspects.

Prioritization Guidelines

Once you have filled in the four categories (new, changing, high-risk, and problematic) on the Worksheet for Identifying Ongoing Competencies (page 25) the next steps are to brainstorm and prioritize the top competencies. Here are some guidelines to help you select those competencies that merit the greatest attention. To keep your competencies program reasonable and achievable, assess 10 or fewer competencies each period.

Guideline #1: Do any of the competencies you have listed on the worksheet appear in more than one box? (i.e., the competency is NEW and HIGH-RISK, or is both CHANGING and PROBLEMATIC.) These will have a higher priority. If it is both HIGH-RISK and PROBLEMATIC definitely make it a priority.

Guideline #2: What are the outcomes (or results) of the competencies listed on the worksheet? If the competency has a large outcome for the patient, customer, or employee, make it a priority. If the outcome is low or small, do not select this item.

Example:

> Competency: Use of a new printer (NEW)
> Patient Outcomes: Low
> Employee Safety Outcome: Low
>
> Competency: Hand washing (PROBLEMATIC)
> Patient Outcome: High (inadequate hand washing can cause sometimes fatal nosocomial infections in patients)

Guideline #3: This guideline specifically helps you prioritize the high risk category of the worksheet. During your brainstorming, some job classifications can generate 10, 20, 30, even 40 high risk items. Unfortunately it is neither cost effective nor achievable to assess such a large list. There are a few methods for identifying which high risk competencies should be selected for a given time period.

One traditional approach to sorting high risk competencies involves using the guideline of *high risk/high volume* vs. *high risk/low volume*. High risk/high volume competencies refer to job aspects that are both high risk and frequent in occurrence. High risk/low volume competencies refer to high risk job aspects that do not happen very often. Perhaps surprisingly, high risk/low volume items are a higher priority than those of high risk/high volume items. The high volume helps us already see a trend in the outcome, whereas low volume represents an unknown that we benefit from monitoring.

I do not prefer or recommend using the high and low volume indicator described above. I instead recommend going a step further. I recommend sorting the high risk category based on which of its elements are **high risk/time sensitive.**

High risk/time sensitive refers to high risk job aspects that need to be performed instantly upon identification. Defibrillator use is a good example. Defibrillator use is high risk because if done incorrectly you can kill the patient and/ or injure employees. When you need to use a defibrillator, you need to be able to perform this skill right away. You do not have time to find and read the policy or the user manual before performing the skill. Therefore, defibrillator use is both high risk and time sensitive.

Using an insulin pump is another example of a high risk aspect of certain job classifications. If you do not program the insulin pump correctly, you can make a patient sicker, put them in a coma, or even cause their death. But while use of an insulin pump is high risk, it is not time sensitive. When you are setting up an insulin pump, you usually have 20-30 minutes to look up the policy, check the manual, and even have a colleague check your work. It is not something that needs to be performed instantly, so it is *not* time-sensitive.

I would not recommend making insulin pump use a prioritized competency, even though some may argue it could be "low volume" as well. Let's say you do select it, and check off on this competency. Chances are, even months later, when the employee may need to perform this skill, they will probably still seek further support. Rather than selecting this competency and checking it off to ensure positive outcome, try this approach instead: do not select it as a competency because it is not time sensitive. Instead make it standard policy/procedure that after setting up and programming an insulin pump, employees have one or two other colleagues check the settings and set-up. This will ensure a stronger outcome for each patient, and help you get your annual (or periodic) competencies down to a manageable, meaningful list.

Guidelines to Prioritizing Competencies—In Review

1. Does the job aspect appear in more than one box on the Worksheet for Identifying Ongoing Competencies?

2. What are the outcomes for each job aspect (for both patient and employees)?

3. Regarding high risk aspects: if the aspect is high risk and time sensitive, make it a strong priority.

The Key to Meaningful, Cost-Effective Competency Assessment

Quality Improvement

Tying competency assessment to quality improvement is the key to creating meaningful, cost-effective, ongoing competency assessment. Competency assessment should start with your organization's vision and goals. Leadership sets the tone and creates an environment that supports individual accountability for competency assessment. Then ongoing competency assessment and quality improvement efforts must be monitored to help create the skills the organization will need in the future to fulfill its vision and goals.

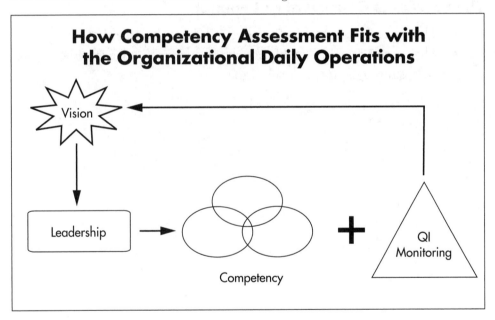

How Competency Assessment Fits with the Organizational Daily Operations

Vision

Leadership

Competency

+

QI Monitoring

Components of a Successful Competency Assessment Program

The Process Includes Initial and Ongoing Assessment

- Initial competencies address new employee needs.
- Ongoing competencies address the changing nature of the job and the work environment.

The Process Is Specific to Each Job Position

- Each job class should have a collection of competencies that are unique to that class.
- Job groups may share competencies with each other (such as competencies that apply to the whole organization or to a department) but should always also include competencies unique to the job group.

The Process Is Consistent but Flexible

- The process has common themes throughout the organization.
- The process remains flexible enough to address the needs of individual groups throughout the organization.

chapter three

Promoting Accountability Through Competency Assessment

- Defining accountabilities for employees and managers

- Competency assessment forms that promote individual accountability

- Documenting competency assessment

- Developing competencies that reflect your organizational needs

Accountability

Competency assessment can only be successful when the accountability expectations of everyone involved in the assessment process are clearly articulated. Both employees and leadership are accountable in the competency assessment process. Their accountabilities should be clearly articulated in policies and consistently supported by organizational actions.

Defining Accountability During the Hiring Process

Competency expectations should be articulated not only to current employees but also to new hires. Articulating these expectations before the person accepts the job can help promote employee buy-in of the competency assessment process at the outset. You may wish to include a paragraph like the one below in your letters to new hires.

> *Upon acceptance of this job, you are expected to participate in our ongoing competency assessment process. As the organization grows and evolves, so will the activities necessary to do your job. We will help you develop the ongoing skills you will need along the way and we invite you to share in this process. Participation in the competency process is a requirement for every employee in our organization. If you would like more information about our competency assessment process or any other aspects of the job, please feel free to contact me.*

Incorporating Accountability into Your Overall Competency Process

In order to make competency assessment truly successful, accountabilities of both employees and managers must be articulated. An example of a competency assessment accountability philosophy that helps clarify and articulate accountability is shown in the following model:

Model for Accountability in the Competency Assessment Process

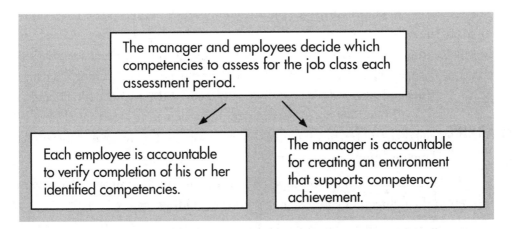

The manager and employees decide which competencies to assess for the job class each assessment period.

Each employee is accountable to verify completion of his or her identified competencies.

The manager is accountable for creating an environment that supports competency achievement.

While the employee is accountable to verify his or her own identified competencies, he or she does not do a "self assessment" per se. Instead the employee is responsible for collecting the evidence that demonstrates his or her individual competency. This puts ownership of competency assessment on each individual in the organization, and takes the manager out of the role of observer or evaluator. Most managers and supervisors take on the role of evaluator of employee performance, when in fact most managers are not in the position to truly evaluate day-to-day competencies. The manager's role should be to establish systems that support competency assessment and to guide the process—not to do assessments for employees. By holding employees accountable for verification of their own competencies, you will not only promote accountability in employees, but you will be able to utilize your managers more productively as coaches and facilitators.

Experience has shown that when managers take on the evaluator role, they tend to create very subjective evaluation systems. With managers evaluating, there is only one opinion guiding the evaluation process. This has the potential to create unfair evaluation and assessment systems—or to create the equally damaging *perception* of unfairness.

By getting the manager out of the evaluator role, you have the potential to create a more objective process. You can create a system that asks the employee to bring evidence of competence (as directed by a predetermined list of acceptable verification methods). The manager is then in a position to monitor the completion of the overall system, but not to be the individual evaluator for a given competency, making the competency process much more objective.

Documenting Competency Assessment

The role of the manager, at the end of the competency period, is not necessarily to verify the employee's skill, but to determine if the employee has successfully completed the competency assessment process using the identified verification methods. The manager then indicates that the employee is "competent," because the employee has successfully completed all the identified competencies, or "not yet deemed competent," which indicates that the identified competencies have not been completed. (Never use the terms "incompetent" in your forms or documentation.)

WARNING

The label "not yet deemed competent" reflects many circumstances that may be seen in the competency assessment process including:

- completing some, but not all, of the competencies identified
- procrastination or resistance to participating in the competency process
- leaves of absence

If the employee is not yet deemed competent, an action plan must be indicated in the employee's record. This action plan should include the actions to be taken by the employee and manager along with a deadline for these actions to be reviewed.

When documenting an action plan that addresses an employee *not* achieving a current "competent" status:

1) The action plan should match the severity of the deficit. For example, if the competency deficit involves patient safety, adjustments of patient care assignment should be addressed in the plan.

2) The action plan should be completed *before* the start of the next competency assessment period.

3) The action plan documentation should include two components—one part of the documentation should address how you (as the manager) are going to support the employee in achieving the action plan, and a second part of the documentation should addressing how you (as the manager) are going to support the organizational mission. This means addressing patient safety issues, financial concerns, assignment or workload adjustments, etc.

The following pages give an example of a competency form that can articulate the competency expectations for a given time period while promoting employee accountability. The first step in the process is to identify the competency priorities for the time period by using the Worksheet for Identifying

Ongoing Competencies in chapter 2. Then write competency statements that reflect the skills identified.

This form (on page 25) uses the skill domains developed by del Bueno (1980) to categorize the competencies identified into the three skill areas: technical, critical thinking, and interpersonal. This is not a requirement in the competency process but does help create a healthy balance in the skill assessment.

Once the competencies are identified, you can begin to determine how you will verify mastery of each competency. While both habit and tradition may lead you to verify through direct observation and marking skills off on a checklist, there are actually 11 different categories of verification methods. (These methods are presented in chapter 4.) You will want to select the verification methods that best reflect the competency skill identified for each competency statement. You will never want to use just one verification method to meet all the competencies identified for a given period, as no single verification method can truly measure all the areas of competency assessment—technical, critical thinking, and interpersonal.

In addition, I encourage you not only to select different verification methods for the competencies identified, but to offer more than one verification option for each competency statement. This way you provide the employee with choices. This strategy will increase employee ownership in the process as employees select the verification methods they prefer from the list of methods identified on the form.

On the next page is an example of one competency statement with several accompanying verification methods that can validate that competency. (These statements can be inserted into the competency assessment form on page 38. The employee is then able to choose from the verification methods listed. All of these methods can demonstrate skills in customer service. By allowing the employee to select the verification method, you give the employee some ownership in the process.)

Competency Statement:	Valid Verification Methods:
Demonstrates the ability to apply customer service principles to everyday work situations.	❑ Submit two customer service peer reviews completed by two different coworkers. ❑ Submit one customer service exemplar based on information from a patient/family member. May include cards, letters, or patient satisfaction information that identifies you by name. ❑ Participate in a case study/discussion group session on customer service. ❑ Complete two customer service case studies.

Creating Competency Forms that Promote Individual Accountability

The format you use to articulate and track competency assessment can also serve to promote individual accountability. The following pages show an example of a format that helps articulate to the employee the identified competencies for a given period and the approved method the employee may select to verify the identified competencies.

This type of competency assessment process holds the employee accountable for a portion of his or her own competency assessment. In this process, the employee is responsible for initiating the competency assessment validation. The manager's role is then to create an environment that encourages and supports this achievement, rather than to merely "check off" or observe the employee's behavior. For example, the manager may identify "customer service" as the competency for the month. The manager can set up the case study/discussion group activities for that month and other activities that support the competency assessment of that skill. This will encourage the employee to participate. If the employee chooses not to participate that month, his or her options will be fewer later on. This is a great way to reward the behavior of motivated, proactive employees. (Many times our competency programs put too much focus on poor performers.) By offering multiple choices early in the assessment period, you will be offering motivated employees a greater variety of choices.

If an employee chooses not to do the competency at all by the end of the assessment period, he or she will be considered "not yet deemed competent." Your organizational policies should articulate the range of consequences for not completing competency assessments as indicated. A good way to develop these types of consequences is to have discussions with other managers about possible responses to different situations. Discuss your "what if this happens?" situations. Describe your worst employee noncompliance nightmares. By discussing these scenarios before they happen, you will begin to see a variety of creative options that can be applied to the variety of situations you will face as managers. Chapter 5 will further discuss the topic of consequences.

Competency Assessment Form for

_____ **through** _____
(job title)   (competency assessment period)

Name _____ Job Class _____ Work Area _____

This form is to be completed by the employee. For each of the competency statements listed below, the employee may select which method of verification he or she would like to use for validation of his or her skill in that area. See the method of verification for details. When this form is complete, submit it to the area supervisor as indicated.

Competency	Method of Verification	Date Completed

For added effect, this form can be catagorized into three domains of skill (technical, critical thinking, and interpersonal).

© Creative Health Care Management • www.chcm.com • 800.728.7766

The following are a list of organizational activities required for this job. Select the method of education/verification that you prefer.

Organizational Education and other Requirements	Method of Education/Verification	Date Completed

This section to be completed by supervisor:

With consideration of the employee's performance and competency assessment, this employee is competent to perform as a/an:

_____ on/in _____   ☐ YES   ☐ NO   (Not yet deemed competent)
(job class)   (work area)

Action Plan:

Employee Signature _____ Date _____   Supervisor Signature _____ Date _____

Competency Forms: Real Life Example

On the following pages you will find an example of an actual competency assessment form developed for the job class of ED Telephone Triage Nurse. Two nurses within the job class of Telephone Triage Nurses and their manager sat down together to decide which competencies to measure for their year-long assessment period. They used the Worksheet for Identifying Ongoing Competencies found on page 25 to identify and select their competencies. These selected competencies reflect the new, changing, high risk, and problematic aspects of the current job as well as the needs of the organization.

This group selected seven competency issues for the year. They reflect the following aspects of the job:

- Problematic aspect of **documentation** reflected in quality improvement (QI) monitors data collected throughout the year
- New patient population of **eating disorder patients**
- New equipment—new complex **telephone system**
- Change in **organizational care delivery** approach—Primary Nursing
- New managed care environment (and **decision-making** related to this changing environment)
- Problematic aspect of **customer service** hospital-wide that was identified through patient satisfaction surveys
- The second phase of a hospital-wide initiative **healthy work environment**

Once the competencies were identified, then verification methods were created to reflect each competency. Several verification methods were created for each competency to give employees a choice. All verification methods were chosen because they both capture the nature of the competency *and* allow for an easy verification process for motivated employees or for employees who already have the skills identified for the job in its current form.

Competency Assessment Form for the ED Telephone Triage Nurse

Name _____ Job Class _____ Work Area _____

This form is to be completed by the employee. For each of the competency statements listed below, the employee may select which method of verification he or she would like to use for validation of his or her skill in that area. See the method of verification for details on completion. When this form is complete, submit it to the area supervisor as indicated.

Competency:	Method of Verification:	Date Completed
Technical Domain:		
Documentation: Regularly uses evaluative statements in charting progress to meet outcomes identified for the patient	☐ Submits two copies of charting that reflects evaluative statements ☐ Attends charting in-service and completes case studies in the class	
Eating Disorder Patient Support: Demonstrates a basic understanding of crisis intervention for eating disorder patients and appropriate interventions to use with these crisis calls	☐ Attends the in-service on "The Basics of Eating Disorders" and completes the case study packet ☐ Completes the Eating Disorder Case Study packet ☐ Completes the Eating Disorder Self Learning packet and exam	
Telephone System: Demonstrates the ability to use the new phone system—including voice mail, conference calling and call-back features	☐ Returns demonstration in telephone class ☐ Peer/Supervisor observation of using the new phone system _Observer's signature_ _____	

Competency:	Method of Verification:	Date Completed
Critical Thinking Domain:		
Care Delivery Initiative (Primary Nursing Implementation): Understands and actively supports the new Primary Nursing care delivery model adopted by the organizations	❑ Completes the Primary Nursing Exemplar ❑ Attends one of the Primary Nursing Focus groups (see newsletter for dates/times)	
Problem-solving and care decisions in managed care: Demonstrates an understanding of resources and options available to patients as the health care environment changes to managed care	❑ Participates in the ED Managed Care discussion groups ❑ Gives a presentation on the options available through the various managed care providers and leads one of the discussion groups.	
Interpersonal Domain:		
Customer Service: Demonstrates the application of customer service principals into the work setting	❑ Compiles two "Customer Service Peer Reviews" from peers or patient/family members ❑ Completes the "Customer Service Exemplar"	
Healthy Work Environment: (Phase 2) Actively participates in creating a healthy work environment as reflected in the Commitment to my Co-worker card and Healthy Work Environments polices	❑ Participates in one of the team face-to-face peer review sessions. ❑ Participates in the written peer review process	

This section to be completed by supervisor:

With consideration of the employee's performance and competency assessment, this employee is competent to perform as a/an:

_____ on/in _____
(job class)   (work area)

☐ **YES**   ☐ **NO**   (Not yet deemed competent)

Action Plan:

Employee Signature _____ Date _____

Supervisor Signature _____ Date _____

Example:
Competency
Assessment
Form
page 3 of 3

Notes

chapter four

Competency Assessment Verification Methods

- Going beyond checklists

- Exploring 11 different ways to verify competencies

- Measuring critical thinking and interpersonal skills

Verifying Competency

Competency verification methods are used to measure the abilities of an individual for a specific competency statement. Competency verification methods include: Tests, return demonstrations, observation, case studies, exemplars, peer reviews, self assessments, participation in discussion groups, presentations, mock events, and quality improvement (QI) monitors.

Competency verification can and should take many forms within the overall competency process. A single method of verification can never effectively capture all three of the domains of skill (technical, critical thinking, and interpersonal.) Therefore a variety of methods should be used to verify the competencies you wish to assess.

Here is a quick three-point quiz to examine your current competency assessment process:

- Do you currently use a collection of checklists to assess all of your competencies?
- Do most of your competency verification methods address only the technical domain of the job?
- Do you wish you could assess more aspects of critical thinking and interpersonal skills?

If you answered "yes" to any of these questions, this chapter will offer you some other options to help you create a competency program that can more accurately assess the skills of the employees in your organization. There is no one verification method that can measure all three skill domains, so you should always use a variety of verification methods in your competency assessment. This chapter describes 11 different categories of verification methods. Some verification methods are better for measuring technical skills, some are better for critical thinking skills, and yet others will help you measure interpersonal skills.

Most organizations only use two to three methods of competency verification. However, 11 categories exist. The two most commonly used verification methods are checklists and test. To measure all of the domains of skill needed to carry out a job, you must go beyond checklists and tests.

- Checklists (observations of skills) are appropriate to measure the *technical* ability to carry out a procedure, but not critical thinking or interpersonal skills.

- Tests can measure the knowledge base individuals possess on a given concept, but not necessarily the application of that knowledge in the real world.
- Not every competency can be observed by an observer.
- Some competencies require reflection on actions taken. Some even require reflection of the choice "not to act" (in situations where not acting was the competent action). Verification methods like exemplars, case studies, peer reviews, self assessments, participation in discussion groups, and other methods can facilitate the assessment of these types of competencies.

Competency Verification Continuum

The different categories of competency verification methods can be placed along a continuum. Measuring *basic skills and knowledge* are on the left side of the continuum and *reflection on actions* falls on the right side of the continuum. Technical skills can often be measured using methods that fall on the left end of the continuum. Critical thinking and interpersonal skills can be measured with methods that fall on the right end of the continuum.

Competency Verification Continuum

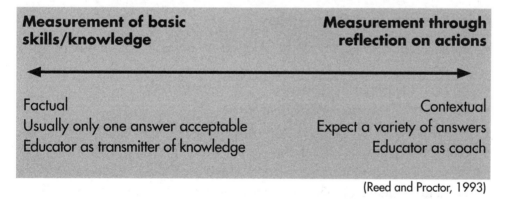

Measurement of basic skills/knowledge	Measurement through reflection on actions
Factual	Contextual
Usually only one answer acceptable	Expect a variety of answers
Educator as transmitter of knowledge	Educator as coach

(Reed and Proctor, 1993)

We are sometimes not as comfortable or familiar with verification methods that fall on the right end of the continuum. These methods rely more on contextual descriptions of performance rather than factual, one-right-answer approaches. Reflections of actions do not rely on a score or number to measure the outcome, but rather written or verbal descriptions of intended or actual outcomes.

Adult Learning Concepts

The most successful competency programs have a strong foundation in adult learning principles. By building your program on adult learning principles, you create a program that supports accountability in employees and respects the employees' freedom to express their individuality in the process.

One key in creating accountability and ownership in the competency process is *to give people choices* in how they carry out the competency assessment process. People have more buy-in to the process if they have some control over the options they can choose from within the process.

In 1929, Eduard Lindeman, in his book, *The Meaning of Adult Education*, indicated his key assumptions of adult learners. One key element: adults have a deep need to be self-directing.

Many of the competency and educational approaches in organizations rely on the educational concepts we were exposed to as children—what some may call "conventional learning." Adult learning principles take a slightly different approach. These principles focus on the aspects that motivate adult learners. Below is a summary of the adult learning principles described by Malcolm Knowles (1980). These principles can be used in your educational activities, as well as in the competency assessment process.

Adult Learning Principles

- Articulate to the learner why he or she needs to know a given skill or information.
- Build on the learner's experiences.
- Encourage the sharing of experiences.
- Provide real-life situations as examples, or have the learner provide them.
- Allow sufficient time for learning.
- Provide a variety of learning methods.
- Use a task-oriented, problem-solving approach to learning.
- Use self-directed learning as a learning option when possible.

(Knowles, 1980)

Incorporating these adult learning principles into your competency program can help create a successful program. Discussions should begin with the managers, educators, and human resources personnel responsible for administering and monitoring your competency assessment program. Discussions and dialogue should also include the executive team or upper management group.

Discuss what outcomes you desire in your overall competency efforts. Discussing these outcomes can help provide consistency throughout the organization, while still allowing individual groups to add specific details to create a program that addresses their unique issues. Identifying these outcome characteristics of your competency program will also help you develop criteria that can be used to periodically evaluate your competency program.

Strong competency programs share these general characteristics:

- an emphasis on outcomes or achievement of performance expectations
- flexibility and adequate time allowed for achievement of outcomes
- use of self-directed activities
- assessment of previous competencies and learning
- use of educator as facilitator and resource
- incorporation of various learning and assessment styles

Competency Verification Methods

There are 11 different categories of competency verification methods. Each verification method will assess and measure a specific skill domain of the job—technical, critical thinking, or interpersonal skills. To truly assess all aspects of the job, you must use a variety of competency verification methods.

Methods of Competency Verification

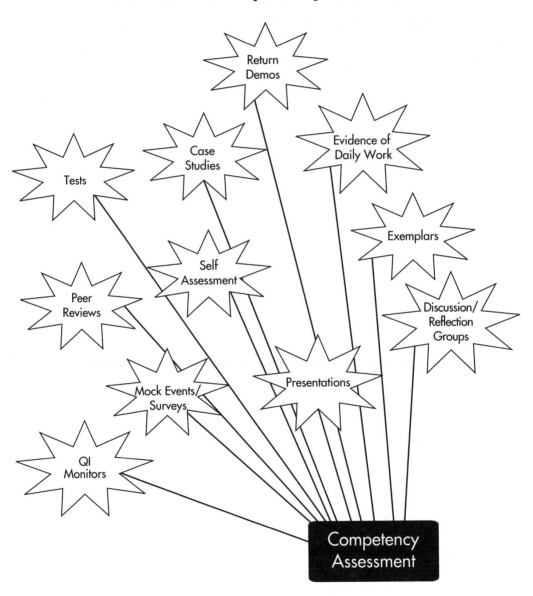

After you identify the competency needs for a job class for your current competency assessment period (see Worksheet for Identifying Ongoing Competencies on pages 25), select verification methods that will effectively assess the type of skill you have identified. Providing several verification methods to measure the same competency is even better, as offering employees several ways to verify their competencies will provide choices to the employees. This approach builds adult learning concepts into your competency program and creates employee buy-in and commitment to the competency process.

The 11 different verification methods are listed below:

- Tests/Exams
- Return demonstrations
- Evidence of daily work
- Case studies
- Exemplars
- Peer review
- Self assessment
- Discussion/reflection groups
- Presentations
- Mock events/Surveys
- Quality improvement monitors

The following sections describe in detail the 11 methods of verification listed above. Each section describes the verification method, then identifies which skill domain the verification best measures, and discusses guidelines for use. Examples of actual verification methods are included in each section. These examples may help you to create verification methods to meet your competency assessment needs.

When creating your overall competency forms, never call this form your competency "checklist". A checklist is just one of the eleven ways to verify your competencies. Checklists fall under the category of return demonstration. You cannot force all you competencies into this one method, nor is it accurate to use the term "checklist" when referring to any of the other 10 verification methods.

WARNING

Tests/Exams

Tests and exams work well to measure cognitive skills and knowledge only. They assess what information people have in their heads.

Tests serve to measure the attainment of cognitive information. Written tests, quizzes, oral exams, surveys, worksheets, calculation tests, crossword puzzle tests, and some forms of word games can all reflect the principles behind the test form of evaluation.

Although tests do a good job of measuring cognitive skills, tests generally do not reflect the behavioral, performance, or psychomotor skills of an individual. Tests are great for measuring an individual's comprehension of basic knowledge related to a particular topic, or for determining whether he or she can cognitively process problems using given formulas or algorithms (for example, medication calculations.) Tests have difficulty, however, measuring behavioral skills such as critical thinking or interpersonal skills. Tests cannot address many aspects of the real world that truly influence the behaviors associated with these skills—skills such as dealing with a difficult customer. You may ask an individual to select the correct response to a situation with a difficult customer from a list of answers. The individual may answer this question right 100% of the time, but may still be unable to carry this action out effectively in a real-world situation.

Tests work best when the desired outcome of the assessment is to measure cognitive knowledge and skill. Ask yourself, "Is retention of information what we want to measure for this competency?" If the answer is yes, then tests are a good choice. However, be aware that sometimes we use tests because we like to feel that we have a concrete way of measuring something. Having a score or numerical value often gives us a sense of security in our measurement of a competency. Do not be deceived by this false sense of security; avoid the trap of feeling that a number is the only way to justify a competency. Competency can and should be measured many different ways, and a numerical score may not always be applicable, necessary, or helpful.

WARNING

Things to Consider When Using a Test as a Verification Method

A common question I am asked related to the use of tests is, "What is an acceptable passing score for a test—75%, 80%, 90%?" My answer is generally this: "It depends on the questions you ask in your test." I do not have a percentage that I use for all tests. For example, if you have a test with 10 questions and the test taker gets questions 1—9 correct, he or she would have a score of 90%. But what if question number 10 covered something that, if not done correctly, could cause someone's death? Then would a score of 90% be acceptable? I think most of us would be uncomfortable with that test outcome. So I generally define test scoring parameters based on the relevance of the questions to the outcomes I am trying to achieve. Sometimes I require a score of 100% as the minimum score for a test. Sometimes I have a combination of parameters. For example, I may require a score of 85% or higher on questions 1—9, and question 10 must be answered correctly (100%) because it involves a life-or-death situation. Make your own judgment for each test based on the overall outcomes you are trying to achieve.

When you identify a competency that requires an outcome of the retention or understanding of information, a test is a great way to validate this type of skill, but remember that tests have their limitations as a competency verification method. Use them wisely.

Example:

This is a great example of a test used to achieve a standard of "providing information" (see page 5) regarding hazardous material.

ENVIRONMENT SERVICES NEW PRODUCT INFORMATION

Be aware of the chemicals you work with.

The following new product is now available on our cleaning carts as a multi-surface cleaner.

Understanding this product will help us provide a safe environment for our customers and ourselves.

Clean-All!

Test what you know about this product

Refer to the HazMat reference book for answers. Answers also posted on the Safety Bulletin Board.

What is it?
Clean-All is a germicidal detergent used to clean surfaces in patient care areas and public spaces.

How is it harmful?
Clean-All may cause _____ irritation.

What special protection do I need to work with this substance?
Wear _____ whenever using this product.
Clean-All may cause skin irritation for some people

What should I do if I am exposed to this substance?

For Eyes

Flush for _____ minutes, and seek medical attention.

If Swallowed

Drink a large glass of _____. Call a doctor. Do not induce vomiting.

NEW PRODUCT REVIEW: CLEAN-ALL

This section must be completed and returned to the Safety Committee. Box 2124 Hospital Mail

Check one:

❑ I have completed the safety worksheet on the new chemical and have no further questions at this time.

❑ I have completed the safety worksheet, but have further questions. Please contact me at _____. (You will be contacted by the Safety Officer or committee member within 72 hours.)

Employee Signature _____ Date _____

Diabetes Mellitus Cross-Word Puzzle

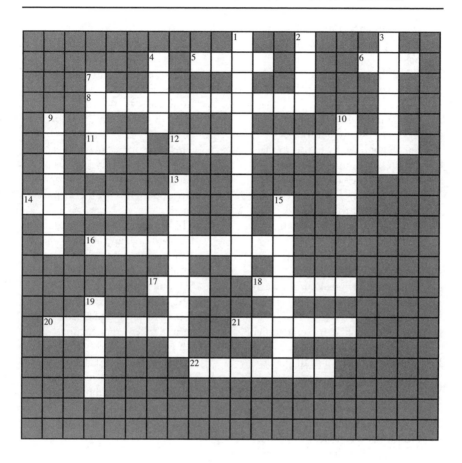

Example:

Diabetes
Mellitus
Cross-Word
Puzzle

(page 1 of 3)

Example:

Diabetes
Mellitus
Cross-Word
Puzzle

(page 2 of 3)

Across

5. This is an important component in maintaining good control of diabetes.
6. This is the type of insulin that peaks in 6–10 hours and lasts at least 18 hours.
8. This can happen to tissue if injection sites are not rotated.
11. You do not have to do this to the site after an insulin injection.
12. This type of hemoglobin test shows how well diabetes has been controlled over a 2–3 month period.
14. Used to treat an unconscious person with diabetes.
16. Always check this date on the insulin bottle.
17. What the body breaks down when glucose is not available for cell energy.
18. Diabetics should carry some form of this with them at all times.
20. When insulin is not available or working as it should, _____ cannot enter the muscle cells, and builds up in the blood stream.
21. A sign of hyperglycemia.
22. This urine test should be done any time the blood glucose is greater than 300, or if the patient feels sick or has signs of hyperglycemia.

Down

1. Signs of this include nausea, vomiting, weakness, lethargy, headaches, heavy breathing, abdominal pain, and high blood glucose levels.
2. Insulin absorption will ____ according to the injection site chosen.
3. This needs to be known, specified, ordered about the type of insulin the patient takes before administering any insulin. It is another name for source.
4. This should be assessed on a daily basis at home and at the hospital.
7. When a long and a short acting insulin are given at the same time, this one is drawn up first.
9. The frequency with which patients should record blood glucose levels, insulin taken, and reactions.
13. Illness usually _____ (increase or decrease) the blood glucose level.
15. A sign of hypoglycemia.
19. The species of insulin or insulin source most used.

Bonus Questions

23. When glucose can no longer enter the muscles cells and builds up in the blood stream, what condition is the result?
24. Exercise _____ (increases or decreases) need for insulin, when the beginning blood glucose level is <240.
25. Name the insulin site which is to be used for most patients ≥7 years of age.

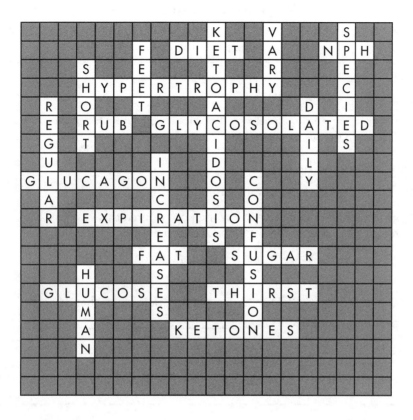

Example:

Diabetes
Mellitus
Cross-Word
Puzzle
(page 3 of 3)

Bonus Answers:

23. Hyperglycemia
24. Decreases
25. Abdomen

Example:

Manager
Competency
Understanding
the ADA

(page 1 of 3)

MANAGER COMPETENCY
UNDERSTANDING THE AMERICANS WITH DISABILITIES ACT
Competency Validation

Competency:

Demonstrates an understanding of the Americans with Disabilities Act and its application to the work setting.

The answers can be found:

◆ in the ADA Manager's Guide from Human Resources

◆ by attending one of the ADA workshops offered this year (see the hospital newsletter for dates and location of the classes)

◆ on the internet at www.usdoj.gov/crt/ada/qandaeng.htm.

1. The Americans with Disabilities Act generally states that disabled persons are entitled to … _____

   _____

   _____

   _____

   _____

   _____

   _____

2. An employer may *not* ask or require a job applicant to take a medical exam before making a job offer, or make any inquires about the nature or severity of the disability. However, the employer *can* ask an individual what two things?

   A.

   B.

3. List three reasonable accommodations employees with disabilities may need the employer to make:

   A.

   B.

   C.

4. When is an employer required to make a reasonable accommodation?

Example:

Manager Competency Understanding the ADA

(page 2 of 3)

Example:

Manager
Competency
Understanding
the ADA

(page 3 of 3)

Answers to Managers ADA Competency Validation:

1) The Americans with Disabilities Act guarantees equal opportunities in public accommodations, employment, transportation, state and local government services and telecommunications. It gives civil rights protection to individuals based on race, color, sex, national origin, age, and religion.

2) A. Employers may ask about an individual's ability to perform specific job functions.

   B. Employers may ask an individual with a disability to describe or demonstrate how she/he would perform particular job functions.

3) Reasonable requests disabled employees may make include:
   –making existing facilities used by the employees readily accessible or usable by an individual with a disability.
   –restructuring the job
   –modifying work schedules
   –acquiring or modifying equipment
   –modifying exams, training or other programs

4) An employer is required to make reasonable accommodations when the disability becomes "known" to the employer. This is usually triggered by a request from the individual with the disability.

For more detail about the answers, refer to the resources mentioned at the top of the ADA Competency Validation.

Return Demonstration

Return demonstrations are great for measuring technical skills.

A return demonstration involves an individual demonstrating a set of skills to a skilled observer. Return demonstrations may occur in an artificial environment such as a skills lab or classroom, or they may occur in real-world settings. Return demonstrations, whether done in an artificial environment or real-world setting, always have one thing in common—there is a **control factor**. In an artificial setting, the control factor is the setting itself. You are removing the employee from the public setting and allowing for safe "mistake-making" to occur.

In a real-world setting, where the skill is being performed in public or on a patient, the control factor becomes the observer of the return demonstration. The observer must be aware of this role of being the "control factor." The duty of the observer is to keep the environment safe. He or she must stop the skill demonstration any time the skill is being performed in an unsafe manner or in a way that may have any negative consequences for the patient, public, or employees.

A return demonstration is usually a planned activity in which an individual is asked to demonstrate his or her skills for the purpose of assessment. Return demonstrations are excellent for verifying competencies that require psychomotor skills. Describing an action is one thing; doing it is quite another.

Examples of skills for which a return demonstration would be an appropriate verification method include:

Clinical:
- Airway bagging techniques
- IV starting skills
- Finger sticking skills
- Lab tests
- Suturing and suture removal
- X-ray procedures
- Cardiopulmonary resuscitation (CPR) procedures

Non-clinical:
- Operating certain types of cleaning equipment (environmental services)
- Demonstrating a restraining hold on a violent individual (security officers)
- Following a recipe or meal preparation plan (dietary food services)

Things to consider when using return demonstration as a verification method:

- Make sure the observers are using a standard set of guidelines or criteria for evaluation. This can be done by using a checklist or by simply using already identified policies for the procedure. You do not have to use a checklist, but you must indicate the set of criteria to be used in the "check-off". This can be a policy, prep poster on the wall, operations manual, etc. (The form on page 65 shows an excellent example of a "check-off" without a checklist.)

  Whatever format you choose, make sure that the observer is aware of the criteria for evaluation and their role in the process. Articulating this expectation to the observers will assure uniform evaluation, and discourage evaluation based on individual preference.

- Use return demonstration in a real-world setting only if it will not harm patients or interfere with patient or public outcomes.

- Return demonstrations can be done immediately following an educational event or instruction, or they can be done at a later time. It is perfectly OK to ask the individual to initiate the return demonstration and seek out the appropriate observer later in a real work situation. This promotes accountability in individuals by asking them to initiate the verification process. (See the verification tool on page 63 for an example of this approach.)

Return demonstrations are an excellent way for an observer to evaluate the technique of the individual. Job functions requiring the proficient use of psychomotor skills can easily and accurately be evaluated using this verification method. However, return demonstrations, whether done in an artificial environment or real-world setting, do not capture certain behavioral and attitudinal responses. For example, you may be able to assess the CPR techniques of an individual, but not his or her timely response to an emergency or any emotional responses that may cause him or her to be unable to perform appropriately (such as the "I froze in my tracks" responses that sometimes occur.) Later in this chapter we will discuss other verification methods such as mock events, quality improvement monitors, and exemplars that can assess these behaviors.

As with any verification method, return demonstrations are a great choice to assess some skills but not others. Return demonstrations are good for measuring technical skills, but cannot measure skills in the critical thinking or interpersonal domains.

IV Starting Return Demonstration
Competency Validation —Insertion of Peripheral Catheters

Name _____ Unit/Clinic _____

Classification _____ Employee ID# _____

Prior to Return Demonstration: **Date and Learner Signature**

1. Successfully complete the IV Class   _____
   or Self Learning Packet "Starting a
   Peripheral IV."

2. Read/Review the IV starting policy   _____
   in the Practice Manual (33.14.2) and
   review the steps to IV starting in
   the Springhouse *Illustrated Manual
   of Nursing Practice* pp. 121-128.

Return Demonstration:

3. When you are ready to perform an IV start, notify a qualified observer to assess
   your return demonstration of skill.

                                           Date and Observer Signature

- Staff with previous experience   1.   _____
  in starting an IV must have one
  observation with a qualified observer.

- Staff with no previous experience starting   1.   _____
  an IV must have three observations with   2.   _____
  a qualified observer.   3.   _____

*All Observers: Please review the "Observer Expectations" on the back of this form before
observing someone on this competency.*

*Observer Qualifications: Anyone who successfully completes the above competency for
Peripheral IV starting. If you do not have someone qualified in your area, contact the Float
Pool. All staff in the Float Pool have been trained and observed.*

Example:

This is a good
example of
an employee
initiated return
demonstration.

(page 1 of 2)

Obsserver Expectations

Example:

Employee initiated return demonstration.

(page 2 of 2)

- Use the IV starting policy (33.14.2) in the Practice Manual or the guidelines for IV starting in the *Illustrated Manual of Nursing* (pp. 121-128) to assess the technique of the person you are observing.

- Maintain safety for the patient at all times.
  —Watch the employee through each step of the procedure.
  —Stop the demonstration of skill at any point when the patient is being put at risk (i.e. if the sterile technique is breached, interrupt the procedure).

- If the individual has successfully completed the IV start, sign and date the competency form. If not, encourage the individual to review the procedure and initiate another return demonstration later.

***Thank you for helping us maintain
quality care for the patient.***

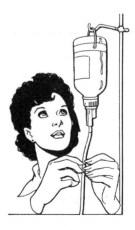

If you have any questions about IV starting or this competency, feel free to call Education Services at ext. 5353.

TECHNICAL SKILLS ASSESSMENT FOR PATIENT CARE TECHNICIANS
Medical and Surgical Units

After completing the basic orientation class or the self-learning packet for each of these items, the PCT (Patient Care Technician) is required to show a return demonstration. When you are ready to do this activity for the first time in your work area, seek out the observer indicated on the form below.

Skill	Required for Completion
A. Foley Catheter Discontinuation *Policy Guideline 12–48*	❑ Observation of Foley Discontinuation by a Nurse _____ *Nurse Signature*
B. Collecting UA/UC from Indwelling Catheters *Policy Guideline 12–48*	❑ Observation of Collecting UA/UC from Indwelling Catheter by a Nurse _____ *Nurse Signature*
C. Hemovac/Jackson Pratt Drain Stripping *Follow Policy Guideline 37–13*	❑ Observation by a Nurse or skilled Paraprofessional* _____ *Nurse or Paraprofessional Signature*
D. Hemovac/Jackson Pratt Dressing Change *Follow Policy Guideline 37–15*	❑ Observation of Hemovac/Jackson Pratt Dressing Change by a Nurse _____ *Nurse Signature*
E. NG Canister Set-up/ Emptying *Follow Policy Guidelines 18–1*	❑ Observation by a Nurse or skilled Paraprofessional* _____ *Nurse or Paraprofessional Signature*
F. Chest Tubes (awareness during patient assistance) *Follow Policy 43–7*	❑ Skills Fair Attendance—Return Demonstration _____ *Instructor Signature*

Example:

This is an excellent example of a "check-off" return demonstration.

(page 1 of 2)

Return Demonstration

Example:

Check-off return demonstration.

(page 2 of 2)

Skill	Required for Completion
G. Trachs (awareness during patient assistance) *Follow Policy Guidelines 45–7*	❑ Skills Fair Attendance—Return Demonstration ———————————————— *Instructor Signature*
H. Suprapubic Catheter Dressing Change *Follow Policy Guideline 58–19*	❑ Observation of Suprapubic Catheter Dressing Change by a nurse ———————————————— *Nurse Signature*
I. Pneumoboots Application *Follow Policy Guideline 73–18*	❑ Self Review of at least one application ———————————————— *Signature*

*A "skilled paraprofessional" is any Patient Care Technician or Nursing Assistant who has worked on the unit for a year or more.

Evidence of Daily Work

Evidence of daily work can measure skills in the technical domain.

Many of the skills we need to verify in individuals are demonstrated every day in the work setting. Assessing the actions we demonstrate on a daily basis to do our job is a valid form of competency assessment. This can also be a highly cost effective verification method because it does not require special time outside the workday.

Here are some examples:

- How can you verify that a secretary knows how to use a given software package on the computer?

  Evidence of daily practice = The secretary submits a document produced using that package (for example, the budget spread sheet or a newsletter).

- We just got a new voice mail and e-mail program in our departments. How do we verify the competency for something like that?

  Evidence of daily practice = Have each person send e-mail/voice mail messages to the others or to a central location.

- We have staff that needs to assemble equipment, food trays, sterile trays, and other items. How do I measure the competency for those tasks?

  Evidence of daily practice = Observe the finished product.

Sometimes observation of daily work is so obvious that we forget to use it as a verification method. Keep in mind that the observer of the finished product or action can be a supervisor, a peer, or a member of another department. By using other team members, you promote team-building.

One of the biggest barriers to using "evidence of daily work" is our ability to capture and document it. The following story is a great example of how one group creatively accomplished this:

> In one hospital the physical therapy and ortho departments were meeting to discuss the purchase of a new type if orthopedic trapeze unit for the patient beds. Their discussion turned to competency assessment—"How are we going to check everyone off for this change in equipment?" You could see a dark cloud

cover the group. They were imagining over 50 return demonstrations for all the nursing assistants and physical therapy assistants. It was an overwhelming prospect.

Then someone suggested, "We should use Evidence of Daily Practice instead of Return Demonstration." Evidence of Daily Work was already measuring the competency of the set-up of the current trapeze unit. Routinely, nurses and therapists check the stability of the unit prior to transferring the patient into bed. So the competence of the assistant was being routinely assessed through daily work. Now they just needed to capture this somehow.

The hospital asked Material Services to change the equipment tracking tag on the trapeze equipment to capture this competency assessment. They added two questions to the tag:

Who set up the equipment for use:_____

Was the setup done correctly? ❏ Yes ❏ No If no, explain_____

_____Signature of Nurse/Physical Therapist

When the equipment was sent back to Material Services, the Material Services personnel would enter the equipment change in the computer. Then, rather than throwing the card away, they would put it in an envelope and send it to the assistant who assembled the trapeze unit.

Voila! Competency of the trapeze unit assemblage is assessed in daily practice and documented with very little effort.

This is a great example of capturing the competency assessment activities already being done in our organizations on a daily basis. It also shows a great way for departments to support each other in developing more effective strategies for meaningful competency assessment.

Case Studies

Case studies are great for measuring critical thinking skills.

Case studies generally provide individuals with a situation and ask them to explain their responses or choices in that given situation.

Case studies can be prepared many different ways:

- Create a story of a patient or work situation. Then ask questions that reflect that situation and capture the nature of the competency you are measuring. When creating case studies, we can sometimes give or lead the employee to the answer without realizing it. We do this by including or not including certain information in the case study. (For example, "A patient enters your emergency department holding his head and clear fluid is dripping out of his nose.")

- Identify questions that capture the nature of the competency you are trying to measure, and have the employees use their real-life situations as the story. Then they can use the list of general questions identified to demonstrate their critical thinking skills in a real-life situation. For example, to measure a competency on being a good steward of our resources when selecting equipment or when selecting supplies to use during a work situation, ask the employee to bring a scenario where they were recently faced with equipment or supply choices. Then use a common set of questions regarding stewardship of resources to ask for their responses.

This second approach to case studies is much better at revealing application to real-world situations. It also helps assess the employees' ability to observe. As they explain the story or situation, they are showing their observation skills. The more they are able to consciously observe, the better their choice in the situation will be.

Case studies can be used alone or shared in discussion/reflection groups for further team-building and group problem-solving. (See the "discussion/reflection groups" section later in this chapter for more examples of this verification method.)

Diabetic/Neurologic Case Study

Elizabeth is a 37-year-old female with insulin dependent diabetes. She was admitted two days ago to the ICU with hyperglycemia and peripheral neuropathy. Blood glucose on admission was 970. She cannot remember when she last took her insulin. She was transferred from the ICU to the Med-Surg Unit today. Information on transfer at 2:00 pm includes:

- Bloodsugar 320
- Insulin pump discontinued 2 hours before transfer
- Loc = Oriented X 3
- Lower extremities test out slightly weak bilaterally

In the evening Elizabeth walks to her doorway and calls to the desk, "Did I leave the oven on? Can someone check?" As you help her back to bed you note her speech is slow. She is also cool and clammy. Her gait is ataxic and she has difficulty getting into bed. Her coordination seems off.

1) What neurological changes are happening to this patient?

2) Is this patient showing signs of hypoglycemia? If so, what are they?

3) What nursing actions would you continue or initiate during your shift with this patient?

Age Specific Aspect:

Would you consider anything different in your actions if this were an 87 year old woman rather than a 37 year old woman?

Example:

This is an excellent example of a case study with an age specific aspect.

Staffing Coordinator
Case Study

Critical Thinking Domain

It is 5:30 Saturday morning; census is 381. There are requests for 39 float nurses and 12 paraprofessionals. All staff currently working are aware of how short staffing is and have already been asked to stay. In fact there are 17 staff people already doubling from the previous shift. Individual patient care units have called all their own staff, doubles and partial doubles have been confirmed and you still have 18 unmet requests for nurses. Some charge nurses have stated that if no more help is available, patient care will not be safe. The shift supervisor looks to you for assistance and direction.

1) What factors do you assess?

2) Remembering your timeline, prioritize your possible interventions and decisions.

3) How do you assess the effectiveness of your actions/decisions?

Example:

Staffing
Case Study.

Case Studies

Ethics
Case Study

Example:

Ethics
case study.

Human Resources Personnel

You are a Human Resources Assistant at your organization. By virtue of your position you are aware of the confidential information that, within the next three months, there will be a major 'layoff' of employees. Your best friend is also an employee of your company, and you have learned that she is on the list of employees to be relieved of their jobs. Your friend is also in the process of purchasing a new home. You are certain that, if your friend had any idea she would soon be losing her lob, she would not even be contemplating the purchase of this larger, more expensive home. If you tipped her off, you would obviously be saving her considerable anxiety later on.

1) What (if anything) would you do?

Pain Management
Case Studies

Two patients are presented. For each patient you are asked to make decisions about pain and medication.

Case Study A

Edward is 30 years old and has been hospitalized following a fractured hip sustained in a skiing accident two days ago. Your assessment yields the following information:

> No history of allergies or chronic illness; receiving vitamins and diet supplements; weight 165; BP = 120/80; HR = 80; R = 18; on a scale of 0 to 5 (0 no pain/discomfort, 5 worst pain/discomfort), Edward rates his hip pain as 4.

1) On the patient's record you must mark his pain on the scale below. Circle the number that represents your assessment of Edward's pain:

0   1   2   3   4   5

No pain/discomfort   Worst pain/discomfort

2) Your assessment, above, is made four hours after Edward received morphine 10 mg. IM. During the 3 hours following the injection, Edward's pain ratings ranged from 3 to 4 and he had no clinically significant respiratory depression, sedation, or other untoward side effects. His physician's order for analgesia is "morphine IM 5 to 15 mg. q3-4h PRN pain relief." Check the action you will take at this time:

_____ a)　Administer no morphine at this time.

_____ b)　Administer morphine 5 mg. IM now.

_____ c)　Administer morphine 10 mg. IM now.

_____ d)　Administer morphine 15 mg. IM now.

3) Is your medication choice, above, determined by your concern that any of the following are likely to occur in this particular patient? Check all that apply.

_____ a)　respiratory depression
_____ b)　addiction (psychological dependence)
_____ c)　tolerance to analgesia
_____ d)　physical dependence (withdrawal)
_____ e)　other; specify
_____ f)　none of the above are major concerns

Example:

This is a good example of reflection included with a case study.

(page 1 of 5)

Pain Management
Case Studies

Case Study B

Frank is 75 years old and has been hospitalized following fractured hip sustained in a fall two days ago. Your assessment yields the following information: history of arthritis and hypertension, receiving antihypertensive and anti-inflammatory medications; weight 150; BP = 150/90; HR = 80; R = 18; on a scale of 0 to 5 (0 = no pain/discomfort, 5 = worst pain/discomfort), Frank rates his hip pain as 4.

Example:

Reflection included with a case study.

(page 2 of 5)

1) On the patient's record you must mark his pain on the scale below. Circle the number that represents your assessment of Frank's pain.

     0   1   2   3   4   5

No pain/discomfort   Worst pain/discomfort

2) Your assessment, above, is made four hours after Frank received morphine 10 mg. IM. During the 3 hours following the injection, Frank's pain ratings changed from 3 to 4 and he had no clinically significant respiratory depression, sedation, or other untoward side effects. His physician's order for analgesia is "morphine IM 5 to 15 mg. q3-4h PRN pain relief." Check the action you will take at this time:

_____ a)   Administer no morphine at this time.

_____ b)   Administer morphine 5 mg. IM now.

_____ c)   Administer morphine 10 mg. IM now.

_____ d)   Administer morphine 15 mg. IM now.

3). Is your medication choice, above, determined by your concern that any of the following are likely to occur in this particular patient? Check all that apply.

_____ a)   respiratory depression

_____ b)   addiction (psychological dependence)

_____ c)   tolerance to analgesia

_____ d)   physical dependence (withdrawal)

_____ e)   other; specify _____

_____ f)   none of the above are major concerns

Pain Management
Case Studies

There is no one right answer to these case studies. However, it is important to examine why you selected the answers you did. Your answers reflect your beliefs and values. Take some time to review your answers based on the pain assessment algorithm and information below.

Reflection for Case study A and B

The major difference between Edward and Frank are their ages. Managing an elder patient's pain can be challenging. Many people don't know the factors that can impede optimal pain management.

Elderly patients are often under-treated for cancer pain according to many studies. Attitudes of health care professionals and the public, as well as our patients themselves, toward pain can impede appropriate care because many people consider acute and chronic pain to be a normal part of aging. In some instances, pain is not assessed because elderly patients, who may be confused, have difficulty communicating their pain to health professionals. In other instances, clinicians have mistaken beliefs about decreased pain sensitivity and heightened pain tolerance in the elderly. Frequently, the elderly are given nonopioids or weak doses of medications because their care providers mistakenly believe that they cannot tolerate opioid agents.

The elderly should be considered an at-risk group for the under treatment of cancer pain because of inappropriate beliefs about their pain sensitivity, pain tolerance, and ability to use opioids. Elderly patients, like other adults, require aggressive pain assessment and management.

Pain management in the elderly presents several challenges, including the discrepancy between the high prevalence of pain in the elderly and the limited attention to this group in the research literature and in medical and nursing texts (Ferrell, 1991). Of all reports about pain published annually, less than 1 percent focus on pain experience or syndromes in the elderly (Melding, 1991). Current pharmacologic research is often limited to single-dose studies in young or middle-aged adults and does not assess the complications and side effects of medications in the elderly. Elderly patients who participate in pain clinics or studies are likely to be the mobile elderly. Furthermore, elderly patients are often excluded from rehabilitation programs and aggressive treatment of pain (Middaugh, Levin, Kee, et al., 1988; Sorkin, Ruby, Hanson, et al. 1990).

Case Studies

Example:

Reflection included with a case study.

(page 3 of 5)

Case Studies

Example:

Reflection
included
with a case
study.

(page 4 of 5)

In spite of the lack of research, there is evidence that the elderly experience more pain than younger people. It has been estimated that the prevalence of pain in those older than 60 years of age (250 per 1,000) is double that in those younger than 60 (125 per 1,000) (Crook, Rideout, and Erowne, 1984). Among the institutionalized elderly, the prevalence of pain maybe over 70 percent (Ferrell, Ferreli, and Osterweil, 1990). Elderly patients with cancer often have other chronic diseases, more than one source of pain, and complex medication regimens that place them at increased risk for drug-drug as well as drug-disease interactions.

Cognitive impairment, delirium (common among the acutely ill elderly), and dementia (which occurs in as many as 50 percent of the institutionalized elderly) pose serious barriers to pain assessment (Kane, Oulander, and Abrass, 1989). Psychometric properties of pain assessment instruments, such as VAS, verbal descriptor, and numerical scales, have not been established in this population. Moreover, a high prevalence of visual, hearing, and motor impairments in the elderly impede the use of these tools. Research on the nursing home population shows that many patients with mild to moderate cognitive impairment are able to report pain reliably at the moment or when prompted, although their pain recall may be less reliable. These findings suggest that this population may require more frequent pain assessment than patients who are not cognitively impaired (Ferrell, in press).

Nonopioid analgesics, including acetaminophen and other NSAIDs, are helpful adjuncts to opioids for cancer-related pain. The risk for gastric and renal toxicity from NSAIDs is increased among elderly patients, however, and unusual drug reactions including cognitive impairment, constipation, and headache are also more common (Roth, 1989). Factors that may contribute to altered side effects in the elderly include multiple medical diagnoses, multiple drug interactions, and altered pharmacokinetics. If gastric ulceration is a concern, NSAIDs with lower gastric toxicity (e.g., choline magnesium trisalicylate) should be chosen. The coadministration of misoprostol should also be considered as a way to protect the gastric mucosa.

Opioids are effective for the management of cancer pain in most elderly patients. In the elderly, Cheyne-Stokes respiratory patterns are not unusual during sleep and need not prompt the discontinuation of opioid analgesia. Elderly people tend to be more sensitive to the analgesic effects of opioids, experiencing high peak effect and longer duration of pain relief (Kaiko, 1980). The elderly, especially those who are opioid naive, also tend to be more sensitive to sedation and respiratory depression, probably as a result of alterations in metabolism and in the distribution and excretion of the drugs. For this reason, the prolonged use of longer acting drugs such as methadone requires caution (Ferrell, 1991).

Elderly people in general have increased fat-to-lean body mass ratios and reduced glomerular filtration rates. Opioids produce cognitive and neuropsychiatric dysfunction through poorly defined mechanism that in part include the accumulation of biologically active metabolites such as morphine-6-glucuronide or normeperidine (Melzaclc, 1990). Opioid dosage titration should take into account not only analgesic effects but also side effects that extend beyond cognitive impairment. Such side effects may include urinary retention (a threat in elderly males with prostatic hyperplasia), constipation and intestinal obstruction, or respiratory depression.

Local anesthetic infusions, including lidocaine or opioids, may result in cognitive impairment if significant drug levels in the blood are reached. Orthostatic hypotension and clumsiness may result from tricydic antidepressant administration and other medications used for pain management and concurrent medical illnesses. Precautions, such as assistance during ambulation, should be taken to prevent falls and fractures.

PCA was shown to be safe and effective for postoperative pain relief among elderly patients (Egbert, Parks, Short, et al., 1990). PCA has not been extensively studied for long-term use in the elderly with cancer-related pain. The use of any "high-tech" pain treatment such as PCA or intraspinal analgesia should be titrated and monitored especially closely because of the elderly patient's increased sensitivity to drug effects (Ferreli, Cronin Nash, and Warfield, 1992).

Example:

Reflection included with a case study.

(page 5 of 5)

"Learning on the Fly"
Manager Case Studies

You are the manager for a group of 40 people. You are preparing to have a performance review with one of the employees you supervise. You see the employee in the hall the day before the review and confirm the time you are meeting. The employee agrees, and briefly mentions she would like to discuss possible leave options based on the new parental leave laws. As you return to your office you realize you have not a clue what the law says or how the organization has responded to these legal parameters. You need to figure this out before your meeting tomorrow at 11:00 AM, so you can at least discuss it with some knowledge. This will require some "learning on the fly."

Example:

"Learning on the Fly" Manager Case Study.

1) What are some of the things you would do to educate yourself?

2) What are some of your resources for this type of issue?

3) What would you do if the employee asked you questions you could not answer?

Submit this case study along with your competency record to your supervisor as indicated.

"Learning on the Fly"
Leadership Case Studies

You are leading a committee that has been asked to implement a new automated machine to do work more efficiently in your area. Your committee members were selected to implement this project because of their knowledge of the service area. No one on the committee has ever implemented a project of this nature, and this will be your first try at something like this as well. Your group is familiar with the service needs, but it does not know how to go about implementing a change of this nature.

1) As the leader of this committee, how would you begin in preparing this group to carry out its assignment?

2) What would you do to prepare yourself for leading this group?

3) What resources would you rely on if your group ran into roadblocks along the way?

Submit this case study along with your competency record to your supervisor as indicated.

Example:

"Learning on the Fly" Leadership Case Studies.

Case Studies

Case Studies

CHARGE NURSE STAFFING SKILLS COMPETENCY
INTENSIVE CARE UNIT (ICU)

This is one method to meet the Charge Nurse Competency. Any unit or individual may develop a method of assessment as long as it meets the criteria for the competency and is approved by your unit education counsel.

Example:

Charge Nurse Staffing Case Study.

(page 1 of 5)

TO COMPLETE THE CHARGE NURSE SKILL WORKSHEET

✦ Familiarize yourself with the staffing policies attached.

✦ Use the worksheet to make staffing assignments for the patient care unit illustrated.

Tips

✦ Don't make it more complex than it is. Only use information given, even if it is sketchy.

✦ In this scenario we have not included the use of paraprofessionals or assigning patients to the Charge Nurse. This is just an exercise in matching staff to patient needs.

CHARGE NURSE SKILL WORKSHEET (ICU)

You are the charge nurse on this ICU. You have 5 patients and 4 staff listed below. Please use the criteria in the staff policies attached and the information below to make your staffing assignments.

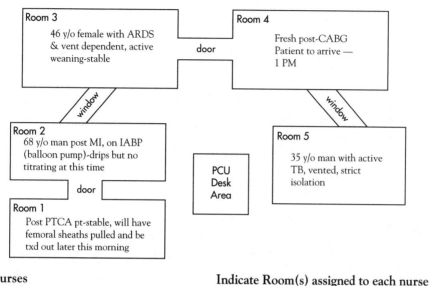

Room 3
46 y/o female with ARDS & vent dependent, active weaning-stable

door

Room 4
Fresh post-CABG Patient to arrive — 1 PM

window

Room 2
68 y/o man post MI, on IABP (balloon pump)-drips but no titrating at this time

door

Room 1
Post PTCA pt-stable, will have femoral sheaths pulled and be txd out later this morning

PCU Desk Area

window

Room 5
35 y/o man with active TB, vented, strict isolation

Nurses

Jeff
- ICU nurse from the float pool
- Has floated to your unit 3 times
- Fully oriented

Jane
- Unit staff nurse for 4 yrs
- IABP certified

Barb
- Unit staff nurse for 3 yrs
- Pregnant

Ann
- Med-Surg nurse floating from med-surg unit
- No ICU training

Indicate Room(s) assigned to each nurse

_____ has successfully demonstrated the appropriate use of staff criteria to match patient care requirements with nursing personnel skill levels.

_____
Date

_____
Competency Reviewer (member of the Charge Nurse staffing task force)

Case Studies

Example:

Charge Nurse Staffing Case Study.

(page 2 of 5)

TITLE	STAFFING ASSIGNMENTS		MANUAL	Policy Manual
AUTHOR:		POSITION:	FILE ALPHABETICALLY WITH SECTION:	
APPROVAL BODY:		CHAIR:	REVIEW DATE:	
			REVISION DATE:	

Example:

Charge Nurse Staffing Case Study.

(page 3 of 5)

POLICY

The Charge Nurse or Nurse Manager is responsible for patient assignment of staff. The following criteria are considered in determining staffing assignments for each shift.

    A. Experience and expertise of available staff

        1. Educational preparation

        2. Qualifications of staff

        3. Orientation completed

        4. Role limitation (including clinical practice limitations of Float Pool staff; see Nursing Services policy)

    B. Patient classification data

    C. Patient care needs/priorities, including patient teaching and discharge planning needs

    D. PCU care delivery system

    E. Infection control parameters

    F. Health status or limitations of staff

    G. Special interests of staff

    H. Availability of support/specialist resources

    I. Patient requests

    J. Geography of PCU

To the extent possible, an RN will make a patient assessment before delegating appropriate aspects of nursing care to ancillary personnel.

Nursing Services staff will be assigned accountability to all patients, even when nursing students are given primary assignments.

REVIEWING AUTHORITY		TITLE	DATE

Other policies that may be helpful
in making staffing assignments

According to policy 33.15 (Infection Control) found in the hospital policy manual:

A pregnant nurse **should not** be assigned a patient who has the following infectious diseases:

Rubella

VZV

Measles

Mumps

Pregnant nurses can be assigned to patients who have:

CMV

HIV

HBV (Hepatitis B)

According to policy "Chemotherapy Administration" found in the Medication Manual:

- Nurses must complete chemo orientation before giving chemo.

- Only RNs on the PCU can administer chemo (nurses floating to the unit can give oral chemo and monitor continuous infusions initiated by an RN on the PCU).

- Pregnant nurses may be assigned to chemo patients. They are at no greater risk than non-pregnant nurses if proper technique is used.

Other ICU information:

- Patients in the ICU should be visually monitored at all times ~ either in person or by EKU monitor.

- Only ICU nurses who have taken and passed the balloon pump exam can care for patients on IABP.

- Nurses floating to the ICU who have <u>no</u> ICU training should be buddied with another ICU nurse, rather than having their own assignment.

Case Studies

Example:

Charge Nurse Staffing Case Study.

(page 4 of 5)

CHARGE NURSE STAFFING
SKILLS COMPETENCY
ICU ANSWERS

Example:

Charge Nurse
Staffing
Case Study.

(page 5 of 5)

Jane must have Room 2 since she is the only nurse scheduled who is certified to take care of patients on an intra-aortic balloon pump.

Ann should be buddied with a nurse having a paired assignment because, having no ICU training, she shouldn't have her own patient assignment.

Room 4 should not be a single assignment to a nurse because the patient isn't arriving until 1 P.M. and the assigned nurse would have no other patients until then.

Jeff and Barb can have any assignments except Room 2.

Exemplars

Exemplars can be used to measure both critical thinking skills and interpersonal skills.

An exemplar is a story you tell or write yourself. It describes a situation you have experienced or may experience. It can describe a rationale you thought about and choices you made in a situation.

Exemplars can assess critical thinking and interpersonal skills that are difficult, or even impossible, to observe. Exemplars are one of the few verification methods that can also assess actions that are *not* taken—especially when "not taking action" is the competency choice in a given situation.

Example:

A venipuncture technician comes to draw blood from a patient. The technician finds the patient crying, and there are several family members in the patient's room. They seem to be discussing some sensitive issues. The venipuncture technician chooses to skip this blood draw and go to the others in the area. When the technician checks back later, the patient is still talking with family members. The venipuncture technician checks the chart for information on the nature of the draw, and discusses with the nurse the possibility of deferring the draw until later.

Very little of this competent action on the part of the venipuncture technician can be observed. But if the employee describes this situation in an exemplar story, we can easily see and assess the critical thinking process used. You could also tell the difference between this situation and one in which an employee is trying to avoid doing his or her job. The rationale for the choices made would be clear.

Exemplars can be used in any job class. They are great for both staff and leadership positions. They are especially great for job classes that require establishing trust with a client, providing customer service, or dealing with sensitive issues.

Here are some examples where exemplars can be used. All these examples are difficult to actually observe. Exemplars can provide a way to verify skill.

Chaplains—Ability to discuss death and dying issues with patients
Social Workers and Counselors—Ability to assess and counsel in abuse cases, rape, or other sensitive patient situations
Managers—Ability of a manager to deal with a problem employee. (This exemplar is best done as a hypothetical situation. It is a great way to prepare the manager for skills needed in the future.)

Exemplars

PRIMARY NURSING EXEMPLAR

This form can be used as a personal exemplar (case study reflecting your performance) or can be used by another individual to provide you with peer review.

Name _____ Unit/Clinic _____

Job Title _____ Date _____

This form reflects my contribution to our primary nursing model through the following competency statement: (Select the one that best describes your role.)

❑ Primary Nurse demonstrates accountability to care delivery through planning and coordinating.

❑ Associate Nurses, paraprofessional caregivers, and clinical specialists demonstrate support to the Primary Nursing model through communication and actions supporting the achievement of patient care outcomes.

❑ Leadership, management, and educators demonstrate accountability to the Primary Nursing model by facilitation of activities that support this practice.

Describe one or more situations that demonstrate your accountability to the Primary Nursing Care Delivery Model. Your description should include one or more of the components of Primary Nursing listed below:

Primary Nursing is carried out when:

✧ the nurse-patient relationship engenders trust, and provides consistency and advocacy.

✧ continuity of care is provided.

✧ there is coordinated and efficient planning for transitions to other sites of care.

✧ there is an explicit plan of care focused on meeting identified outcomes.

✧ effective communication within the health care team occurs.

✧ the patient and family are involved in the planning, implementation, and evaluation of care.

Example:

Primary Nursing Examplar.

(page 1 of 3)

Use this space to describe a situation that demonstrates your contribution to our Primary Nursing Care Delivery Model: (Check out the examples on the next page to get yourself started.)

Example:

Primary Nursing Examplar.

(page 2 of 3)

Completed by: self or peer *(indicated below)*

❏ Self _____

Signature

❏ Peer _____

Signature

Submit this case study along with your competency record to your supervisor as indicated.

Some samples to get you started:

Last week I was caring for Mrs. F., a rehab patient. In the Kardex I read the care plan written by the primary nurse. It said we needed to increase her fluid intake over the next few days. As the NA, I have been assisting Mrs. F. with her meals. She has a tough time holding a glass. She does better with a mug. She can even pick up a mug by herself. I have been setting up a mug full of water or juice every 2 hours for Mrs. F. This encourages her to drink a little all day. I also wrote that she handles a mug better than a glass in the Kardex for the primary nurse and other caregivers.

Mary Lipton, NA

Example:

Primary Nursing Examplar.

(page 3 of 3)

I decided to be the primary nurse for Mr. C. after I took care of him after surgery. I found out his wife had just passed away only three months before, and I had a feeling he would not be able to return home on his own. The first day after surgery I called the social worker to make them aware of Mr. C.'s need for transitional care or possibly home care. I met Mr. C.'s son the 2nd day post-op. He was very happy I was exploring ways to provide help after discharge. With his mother's sudden death, he was concerned about his father's care at home. I arranged a meeting with the son, SW, MD and myself. I know the doctors were planning to discharge him soon and there was a lot of planning to do. I also asked the associate nurses for their input. We concluded that Mr. C. should go home with visits from a home health aide.

Sally Adams, RN

Customer Service
Exemplar

An exemplar is a story you tell or write about what you did. Please share your story about how you supported our customer service principles this year. Your customer may be the patient, family, visitors, or a fellow employee. It will vary depending on where you work.

Our customer service principles include:

- Treating the customer with kindness and respect.

- Calling the customer by name, and showing genuine interest.

- Listening to what the customer has to say.

- Helping the customer get the help they need. (Avoid saying, "That's not my job." Instead say, "Let's find someone who can help you.")

Your Name _____ Date _____

Dept./Work Area _____ Job Title _____

Share your story in this space. It does not have to be long. Examples of other stories are found on the back of this form.

Submit this case study along with your competency record to your supervisor as indicated.

Example:

Customer
Service
Examplar.

(page 1 of 2)

Exemplars

Example:

Customer Service Examplar.

(page 2 of 2)

Customer Service Exemplar written by a social worker
(The patient is the customer)

I was visiting a patient the other day in their hospital room. During our visit, the patient said they needed help getting up to the bathroom. I told the patient, "I'm not sure about your restrictions, or the best way to help you, so I am going to quick check with the nursing staff. I will be back in two minutes. I smiled and went to find some help. I found the charge nurse and asked for help. Together we went back to the room and looked at the chart to see the patient needed at least one person to walk with her, and her urine needed to be measured. I helped walk her to the bathroom and the charge nurse set up the urine collector in the toilet.

Customer Service Exemplar written by a volunteer
(A visitor is the customer)

I was on my way to lunch when a visitor stopped me in the hallway and said "Where is the cholesterol screening being done today?" Well, I had no idea where it was, but I said to the visitor, "I'm not sure, but let me take you to the information desk. They can probably help us find out where it is today."

Customer Service Exemplar written by a computer support person
(A fellow employee is the customer)

I got a call from Sarah, a nurse manager, who just hired a new employee and needed to get him into computer training. I asked Sarah if this was the first employee she had sent to computer training, and she said yes. Then I said, "I will e-mail you the steps you need to do to assign a computer ID and get the employee into training. If you have any questions, Sarah, just give me a call or send me an e-mail. I'm here to help."

Building Bridges Exemplar

We need to break down the walls between groups and departments—and begin to build bridges.

Through patient surveys and observation of our daily work in our organization, it is evident that we have built a few walls between groups. Some people have described us as a group of silos. We are all working hard in our areas, but not communicating or collaborating as well as we could with other groups and departments. We need to make an effort to change this. *We need to start building bridges.*

Take some time and energy this year to build a bridge somewhere. Here are some ways you can achieve this:

☆ Get to know someone in another department. This can be done in person or over the phone. The next time you talk with someone regarding your daily business, call them by name, ask them how their day is going, and thank them for their support.

☆ Include other groups in committee or group work. Think of other groups or departments that may benefit from the work issues to be addressed. Don't just tell them about it "after the fact." Partner with them from the beginning.

☆ Integrate these ideas into your daily conversations. The way we communicate can keep many walls between us. Watch for statements like, "That's their problem." Instead we should ask, "How can I support you as you address this problem?"

No matter where we work or what our role is, we all need to have the skills and the willingness to help build bridges. Please describe below one situation this year where you made an effort to build a bridge.

Your Name _____ Date _____

Submit this form along with your competency record.

Example:

Building Bridges Examplar.

Examplars

Competency Exemplar
Dealing with Paradox

A paradox is something that seems to be contradictory. Leaders deal with paradoxes everyday. Finding a balanced solution to the paradox is key to successful leadership. Some common leadership paradoxes follow.

- ○ Being tough and compassionate
- ○ Being empathic and objective
- ○ Being able to lead and follow simultaneously
- ○ Being an individual contributor and a team player
- ○ Being self confident and appropriately humble
- ○ Finding agreement in conflict

All of these require a leader to see the larger purpose and exercise critical thinking skills. To demonstrate your efforts in 'Dealing with Paradox', share a situation where you found yourself in a paradox.

- ◆ Briefly share your paradoxical situation.
- ◆ Explain whether you would do anything different if that situation occurred again.

Example:

Dealing with Paradox Examplar.

Completed by _____ Date _____

Submit this form with your competency record as indicated.

Competency Exemplar
Learning on the Fly

Learning is a lifelong process. We need to become comfortable with learning as we go. Take some time to reflect on your learning skills.

Learning on the fly requires us to:

○ Learn quickly when we are faced with new problems and challenges.
○ Be open to change.
○ Initiate our own education or learning.
○ Analyze both successes and failures for clues to improve.
○ Try new solutions to problems.
○ Enjoy the challenges of unfamiliar tasks.
○ Search for the underlying structure and essence of the situations we encounter.

Please share an experience you have had this past year that demonstrated one or all of these concepts required to "Learn on the Fly."

Example:

Learning on the Fly Exemplar.

Completed by _____ Date _____

Submit this form with your competency record as indicated.

Examplars

Examplars

Example:

Managing with
Vision and
Purpose
Leadership
Examplar.

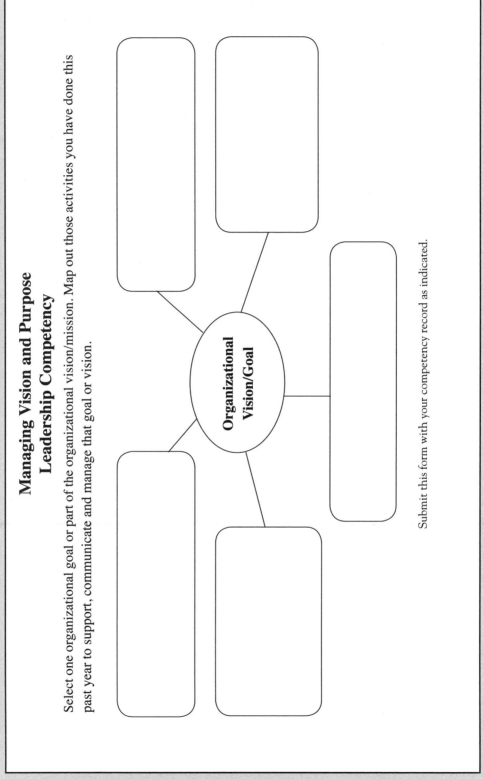

Managing Vision and Purpose Leadership Competency

Select one organizational goal or part of the organizational vision/mission. Map out those activities you have done this past year to support, communicate and manage that goal or vision.

Organizational Vision/Goal

Submit this form with your competency record as indicated.

Peer Review

Peer review can be used to measure interpersonal skills, as well as critical thinking skills.

Peer review is a very powerful tool to help reinforce the behaviors we would like to see in our teams. Peer review can be a positive, motivating experience or it can be a devastatingly negative experience. It all depends upon how it is approached and carried out. When filling out a peer review form, we often ask, "How will my response affect my relationship with this person?"

Below are a few tips to help you create effective, respectful peer reviews.

There are two types of peer reviews: written and face-to-face. Both can provide a great deal of support and encouragement to an employee if carried out in a respectful, well planned way. If your group has never done peer review before, start with written peer review. Face-to-face peer review can be very intimidating, especially if your group has never experienced success with peer review in the past.

To create a healthy approach to whichever peer review approach you take, keep the following three aspects in mind.

The peer review process must be:

- safe for the person *giving* the feedback.
- safe for the person *receiving* the feedback.
- safe for the person who is going to help *interpret* the feedback (this is usually a manager or supervisor).

Once you have created a peer review form or process that is safe for everyone involved, you will need to prepare the group to participate in the process. I generally recommend at least two events where you discuss the intent behind the peer review process and confirm with your group that the process has truly met the "safety" aspects listed above.

Take the time to have these discussions with your group. Do not just stick peer review forms in a mailbox or locker. You are asking for trouble if you do this.

WARNING

Here are a few additional things to consider with peer review:

- Keep the peer review short and to the point. It is usually measuring a single competency item. It is not meant to be a personality profile of an individual, just a measure of a particular interpersonal or critical thinking competency.

- Peer review cannot measure all aspects of the job, only those aspects that are seen by other people. For example, it is difficult for a peer to assess skills in patient education. Patient education is often done alone with the patient and not seen by a co-worker. A co-worker may see documentation, but not the education itself.

- "Peers" used to do peer review are not always people in the same job category. A peer is anyone who sees you do your job. For example, in an operating room (OR), the peers for an OR technician may not be other OR technicians, but instead the scrub nurse, circulating nurse, surgeon, or other personnel in the OR suite they are working in that day.

Peer Review

COMMUNICATION ASSESSMENT
PEER SURVEY

Many skills are required to successfully carry out any job. Communication is one of those skills. This survey is designed to provide feedback to employees on their communication skills.

(See some of our communication goals on the back)

Employee's Name _____

Dept./Work Area _____ Job Title _____

When I am talking with this employee:

	Agree			Disagree	
1. I feel he/she is listening to what I say	1	2	3	4	5
2. I feel he/she speaks honestly and directly to me	1	2	3	4	5
3. I feel this individual makes an effort to clarify differences.	1	2	3	4	5

Comments:

Your Name _____ Date _____

Dept. _____ Job Title _____

Example:

Communication Peer Review

(page 1 of 2)

Peer Review

97

Here are some helpful hints in assessing communication competency and supporting growth of healthy responses:

■ Speak for yourself, and use "I" statements whenever possible.

Example: "I feel left out when you don't communicate the updates you have."

That's much better than "You never tell us what is going on."

■ Listening respectfully involves clarifying and reassuring the person that you have heard them.

Example: "So you are saying that you feel…"

Example:

Communication
Peer Review

■ Listening respectfully does not mean that you agree with the individual. It only means you understand what they are saying to you.

(page 2 of 2)

Communication is an art. There can be lots of different interpretations to one event. Successful communication focuses on demonstrating respect for ourselves and each other regardless of the opinions we may hold.

Dealing with Ambiguity
Leadership Competency Assessment
Peer Review

As a colleague, I value your opinion of my performance. Please take some time to share your thoughts. When you are done, please send this form to _____ by _____ (date)

Employee Name _____ Peer Completing Form _____

Dept./Title _____ Dept./Title _____

Date _____

Based on your observation and interactions with the employee above, please answer the following questions. This information will be compiled with others to assist the employee and supervisor in reinforcing and improving skills related to dealing with ambiguity.

This Individual...	Agree				Disagree
1. can effectively cope with change.	1	2	3	4	5
2. can shift gears comfortably.	1	2	3	4	5
3. can decide and act without having the total picture.	1	2	3	4	5
4. isn't upset when things are up in the air.	1	2	3	4	5
5. doesn't have to finish things before moving on.	1	2	3	4	5
6. can comfortably handle risk and uncertainty.	1	2	3	4	5

Comments:

Thank you for your feedback.

Peer Review

Example:

Dealing with
Ambiguity
Leadership
Peer Review

99

Example:

Customer
Service
Peer Review

Peer Review

Customer Service
Peer Review

Please briefly describe the customer service you observed or received from your co-worker.

Our customer service principles include:

☆ Treating the customer with kindness and respect.

☆ Calling the customer by name, and showing genuine interest.

☆ Listening to what the customer has to say.

☆ Helping the customer get the help they need. We avoid saying, "That's not my job," and instead say, "Let's find someone who can help you."

Employee's Name _____

Dept./Work Area _____ Job Title _____

✎ Briefly describe how this employee contributed to good customer service:

Your Name _____ Date _____

Dept./Work Area _____ Job Title _____

Coping with and Managing Change
Peer Review Worksheet

This form may be used to verify your competency related to "coping with and managing change." Managing change is a skill that we will all need to survive the changes occurring in health care today. Give this form to a peer and ask him or her for feedback related to your skills in coping with and managing change.

	Never	Rarely	Sometimes	Frequently	Always
1. When confronted with a new idea, this individual reflects on the idea before responding.	1	2	3	4	5
2. When a system or issue needs changing, this person is comfortable collecting information about the problem and its possible solutions.	1	2	3	4	5
3. Most of the time this individual appears to have energy to cope with the fast-paced change occurring around him or her.	1	2	3	4	5
4. This person accepts responsibility for his or her personal response to the change.	1	2	3	4	5
5. This person accepts accountability to educate him or herself in becoming more comfortable with the change process.	1	2	3	4	5
6. This individual accepts responsibility for how to share his or her discomfort with the difficult parts of change—for example, knowing when, where, and how to appropriately share or discuss issues.	1	2	3	4	5

Total = _____

Person being reviewed _____ Peer completing the review _____

To the individual being assessed:

Total up the numbers you circled for each statement. If your total is between 21–30, you are doing great. Keep up the good work. If your total is between 11 and 20, you have made a great start. Keep it up. If your total is between 0 and 10, we appreciate your honesty, and encourage you to participate in one of the "Managing Change" activities offered throughout the year.

Peer Review

Example:

Coping with Managing Change Peer Review

Cardiopulmonary Services
Health Team Member Peer Review

Cardiopulmonary Services Practitioner _____

1. How does this co-worker maintain a professional attitude in interactions with patients and health care workers?

2. How are you aware that this co-worker understands the technical and theoretical aspects of Respiratory Care including (but not limited to) respiratory anatomy and physiology, respiratory care equipment, respiratory pharmacology?

3. How does this co-worker provide an atmosphere of trust, respect, and effective communication towards patients and their families?

4. How does this co-worker show responsibility for effective planning and organization? Does he or she utilize appropriate resources to solve problems?

5. How does this co-worker strive for effective communication and good relationships with other members of the health care team?

Peer Review

Example:

Team Member
Peer Review

Partners in Practice
Competencies for Success

Successful partnerships in care delivery require the following elements:

- open and honest communication,

- support from leaders and non-partnered staff,

- recognition of the unique skills we all bring to partnerships regardless of job title or levels of educational preparation.

As part of the team carrying out "Partners in Practice," we need to each demonstrate our ability to contribute to quality care through partnerships.

Each member of the unit must complete the following Partners in Practice Competency by _____ (date)

Competency Statement	Verification Method (select one)	Date Completed
Individual actively participates in the promotion and implementation of partnerships for successful care delivery.	❑ Have two peers complete the Partners in Practice Competency Peer Review ❑ Participate in one of the Partners in Practice Competency Discussion Groups (See _____ for dates and times.)	

Peer Review

Example:

Partners in Practice Peer Review

(page 1 of 3)

Partners in Practice Competencies
Peer Review

Name _____

Unit/Clinic/Area _____   Job Title _____

Peer completeing form _____

Unit/Clinic/Area _____   Job Title _____

Please select one of the following statements that best reflect the aspect of Partnering you are assessing:

❑ participate as a partner in a partnership

❑ support partnerships (even when they themselves are not in a partnership that shift)

❑ support partnerships through leadership, education, and/or communication

Please describe below how this person supported and/or hindered the following ideas behind partnership:

• Uses open, honest communication (not engaging in backbiting, bickering, or blaming)

• Recognizes and uses the unique talents of team member regardless of job title or educational preparation

• Supports and contributes to partnership whether they are in the partnership or not

• Shares the work rather than focusing on dividing it equally

• Celebrates successes in delivering patient care together

Example:

Partners in Practice Peer Review

(page 2 of 3)

Example:

Partners in
Practice
Peer Review

(page 3 of 3)

Peer Review

*Thanks for taking the time to provide feedback to help
us achieve our care delivery goals.*

Please return this peer review to _____ by _____

Self Assessment

Self assessment can measure some critical thinking skills, especially those associated with values and beliefs.

Self Assessment is a verification method that is sometimes avoided. Some people feel it is not a valid form of verification, so they do not use it at all. Other organizations tend to use it to measure everything. Overuse of self assessment is especially common during orientation. New employees are asked to assess all their new skills on an orientation checklist. Neither of these approaches really utilizes this verification method in the way that best fits its purpose.

Self assessment is a valid form of competency assessment when applied to the appropriate competencies. Self assessment is best used to assess aspects of the affective domain of learning. The affective domain includes those things such as values, beliefs, opinions, and attitudes. Self assessment engages the individual in a reflective exercise that allows him or her to explore some of the thoughts that influence day-to-day judgments. Just completing this form of verification has merit. It allows employees to reflect on and put into words their conscious and previously unconscious thoughts.

A self assessment verification tool should provide guidance to assist individuals in understanding the purpose of the verification tool and how to complete it. Not only can some self assessment tools help individuals judge their own competency level, but those tools can guide the individual to the appropriate actions to meet the required competency outcome level.

Self assessment can be a very valuable verification method for selected competencies. It is especially valuable in measuring competencies that relate to values, beliefs, myths, and assumptions that may help or hinder us in achieving our desired work-related outcomes. Self assessment has its place. Do not overuse it; do not overlook it.

An example of a case study that can also be used as a self assessment verification is the Pain Management Case Study found on page 108.

Coping with and Managing Change
Self Assessment Worksheet

This form may be used to verify your competency related to "coping with and managing change." Managing change is a skill that we all need in order to survive the changes occurring in health care today. Take some time to reflect on the skills you need to deal with change.

	Never	Rarely	Sometimes	Frequently	Always
1. When I am confronted with a new idea, I reflect on the idea before responding.	1	2	3	4	5
2. When a system or issue needs changing I feel comfortable collecting information about the problem and possible solutions.	1	2	3	4	5
3. Most of the time I feel I have enough energy to cope with the fast-paced change occurring around me.	1	2	3	4	5
4. I accept responsibility for my personal response to the changes around me.	1	2	3	4	5
5. I accept accountability to educate myself in becoming more comfortable with the change process.	1	2	3	4	5
6. I accept responsibility for how I share my discomfort with the difficult parts of change. For example, I know when, where, and how to appropriately share or discuss.	1	2	3	4	5

Total = _____

Total up the numbers you circled for each statement. If your total is between 21 and 30, you are doing great. Keep up the good work. If your total score is between 11 and 20, you have made a great start. Keep it up. If your total is between 0 and 10, we appreciate your honesty, and encourage you to participate in one of the "Managing Change" activities offered throughout the year.

> Contact for Information:

Your Name _____   Date _____

Submit this form with your competency assessment record.

Self Assessment

Example:

Coping with and Managing Change Self Assessment

Example:

Pain
Management
Self Assessment

(page 1 of 3)

Pain Management Self Assessment Worksheet

The ABCDE process is the recommended clinical approach to pain management from the AHCPR Standards. Take some time to review your pain management practices with this process. Answer the questions based on a patient you are caring for or have cared for in the past. Assess your own competency regarding pain management by combining your patient assessment with those on the algorithm attached to this page. This is also a great discussion group tool.

		Questions to ask	Reflect on your patient care
A	Ask and Assess	• How often did you ask about their pain? • Did you assess pain systematically? For example, did you use a hierarchy of assessment techniques? • What intervals did you find suitable to assess pain after the intervention? (for example, 15–30 minutes after IV drug or 30 minutes after oral drug or hours after non-drug interventions) • Did you reassess the patient with each NEW report of pain?	
B	Believe the patient	• Did you believe the patient's self-report of pain? • How did you convey your belief of the patient regarding pain and experiences affecting their pain?	

Pain Management Self Assessment Worksheet (continued)

		Questions to ask	Reflect on your patient care
C	Choose appropriate interventions	• How have you used different pain control options that are appropriate for this patient in this setting?	
D	Deliver interventions	• How have you delivered/coordinated interventions to reflect a timely, logical, coordinated approach to pain management?	
E	Empower patients and families	• How have you enabled patients to control their course of pain management as much as possible?	

Self Assessment

Example:

Pain
Management
Self Assessment

(page 2 of 3)

Self Assessment

Example:

Pain

Management

Self Assessment

(page 3 of 3)

Algorithm of
Pain Assessment Techniques

Purpose of Competency Assessment

- To provide a mechanism for directing and evaluating the competencies needed by our employees to provide quality health care services to our customers.
- Identify areas of growth and development, and provide opportunities for ongoing learning to achieve continuous quality improvement.

Can the patient report pain?

Yes

No

Communication impaired secondary to confusion, mental retardation, stroke, mechanical ventilation, sedation, etc.

Patient's Self Report

Ask the patient about:

- location of pain(s)
- intensity/severity of pain
- quality of pain: sharp, dull, shooting, etc.
- aggravating/relieving factors
- effect on sleep
- patient's goals of pain management

Behavioral Signs

Are there reasons why behavioral signs cannot be displayed?

Yes

No

secondary to neuro deficits, unconscious, sedated

Physiological signs

↑ Heart rate
↑ B/P
Sweating
Dilated Pupils

Observe

Facial grimacing

↑ muscle tension

Body movements (guarding, writhing, flailing)

Vocalizing: crying moaning, screaming

Warning: Discrepancies may occur between the three realms of assessment data. These discrepancies may result from several factors, including physiological adaptation to pain, coping skills acquired by patient, social/cultural expectations of behavior. **"The single most reliable indicator of the existence and intensity of acute pain of pain is the patient's self-report."** (AHCPR, Clinical Practice Guidelines, 92-0032, 11.)

Discussion/Reflection Groups

Discussion and reflection groups can be used to measure critical thinking skills (and when linked with mock events, may also be able to measure technical and interpersonal skills).

Discussion groups are a valid way to look at critical thinking skills, as well as to promote group cohesiveness and mutual support. The purpose of a discussion group is to allow a group of individuals to share their thoughts and strategies on an issue, and discuss the merits and consequences of each aspect.

Some examples of discussion/reflection groups are

- debriefing session after a code
- debriefing session after a mock event/disaster
- discussion group using a hypothetical situation
- discussion group to analyze a sentinel event

Discussion groups often use the strategies outlined in a case study, but go beyond the individual analysis of the situation to a group process of problem solving. In discussion groups the individual is asked to analyze a situation and the group is asked to discuss and evaluate the choices presented. When used for competency assessment, discussion groups should have a facilitator. Discussion groups are a verification method that should be well planned. The discussion itself can be a planned event or spontaneous, but the competency criteria should be prepared and clearly identified prior to the discussion.

To successfully use discussion groups as a verification method, you should have a facilitator. A facilitator is someone in the group who takes responsibility for overseeing the discussion and guiding the process. The facilitator should articulate the expectations of the competency and the use of discussion groups as a verification method. Also the form of evaluation should be described and discussed. Discussion groups are a purposeful event and the participants need to be aware of this.

Measuring critical thinking skills may not be familiar to or easy for many groups and group facilitators. Here are a few strategies to help assess critical thinking competencies using discussion groups:

- Use a facilitator to guide the group through the process.
- Establish criteria or goals for the discussion activity.
- Select a case study that has meaning to the group. See the section on case studies for some examples. You may also have people share a situation they have recently encountered with the group (for example,

dealing with a difficult customer or situation).

- Identify some questions you will ask about the situation based on your organization's goals and philosophies.
- Competency assessment verification may be done by the facilitator or the group as a whole. Using the group to assess critical thinking skills builds a context for that behavior to continue outside the group. It is important to prepare the group to do this. Set participant expectations and include some activities on giving and receiving feedback in a healthy, respectful way.

Here are some guidelines for participants in a discussion/reflection group:

- Establish expectations of the discussion group prior to the activity.
- Each individual is responsible for any preparation needed prior to the discussion (read and answer case study questions).
- Participants will contribute in the group discussion by sharing their ideas and discussing the merits and consequences of their responses and the responses of others. (If the individuals choose not to participate in the actual discussion during the activity, they cannot use this activity as a measurement of competency verification. They are now only auditing the event.)
- Each individual will commit to providing a respectful environment for group discussion and support the group as a whole.
- Each individual will look for ways to support his or her colleagues in the process.
- Encourage the group to establish action plans for ongoing group support strategies and growth opportunities.

Evaluation of the discussion/reflection activity should be done by the group, if they have been prepared and educated to do this. The art of peer evaluation does take some time to develop, but is well worth the investment. If the group is unable to do this evaluation, or has difficulty carrying it out in some situations, the facilitator must be prepared to function as evaluator. Select only facilitators who can assume this role if needed.

In addition, if the group is able to evaluate their own outcomes of the discussion, the facilitator still has a final evaluation role. When the group comes to their conclusion of overall group performance in the discussion, the facilitator has the final decision to accept or reject this evaluation. Make this part of the facilitator role known to the group prior to starting the discussion/reflection group activity.

The facilitator may reach the conclusion that he or she does not agree with the group's final decision. This can happen two ways:

- The group feels that they met the criteria as a group, but the facilitator believes that the majority of the group *did not* meet the identified criteria.
- The group feels they met the criteria as a group and the facilitator believes that the majority of the group did meet the identified criteria—but that one or more individuals did not reach the goal or there was a significant issue with certain responses they gave during the discussion.

In light of these situations, the facilitator must be prepared to respond. The facilitator can present his or her final conclusion of the group evaluation publicly with the whole group or privately address it with an individual after the event. Either way the facilitator gives the final endorsement of the group decision.

Documentation of discussion/reflection group activities:

Once you have done a discussion group activity for the purpose of verifying a particular competency, and the group and facilitator have agreed that the group met the identified criteria, the event must then be documented. Documentation can be very simple. Take the list of criteria identified and indicate on this form that you used a discussion group to identify the above criteria. Then make a statement that indicates group and facilitator endorsement, and have everyone sign this sheet of paper. Make a copy of this form for each individual, so they can submit it with their other competency evidence at the end of the competency assessment cycle.

These simple strategies can help create a successful verification activity for critical thinking competencies. It can enhance group dynamics and promote ongoing communication among team members. Critical thinking competencies have always been difficult to assess. Discussion groups are one strategy to address this competency.

As a bonus, discussion/reflection groups not only can assess critical thinking skills, but can also help *build* critical thinking skills in your team. Discussion/ reflection groups, as a competency verification method, can be a lot of work, but in our efforts to build strong critical thinking teams, they can be well worth the effort.

Communication Assessment
Case Study/Discussion Group Tool

This competency tool can be used alone as a case study, or as a case study that helps facilitate group discussion. Group discussion allows for a supportive way to assess competency regarding communication skills. Allowing peers to discuss and give feedback to each other on potential responses helps assess skills and supports growth of new communication skills.

Describe a situation involving communication that has occurred recently that caused you to feel uneasy or frustrated.

If you were in this situation...
How could you show to the individual(s) in this situation that you were listening to them?

In what way could you provide direct, honest and respectful feedback or communication?

Describe some ways you could respectfully clarify differences or show disagreement?

Submit this form with your competency record to your supervisor.

Discussion/Reflection

Example:

Communication Discussion Group Tool

Partners in Practice Competency
Discussion Group Activity

Instructions:

1. Attend one of the discussion group sessions to discuss the following topic related to partnership and care delivery.

2. Share with the group your observations and experiences related to your recent partnership experiences along with ways you can help improve or support the desired outcomes.

As you begin the discussion, keep in mind that:

- *We will support the Commitment Card[1] philosophies as we discuss our thoughts.*
- *We do not have to agree with each other.*
- *We will look for ways to strengthen our relationships.*
- *The discussion will focus on our relationships and professional behavior, and not on the division of tasks and assignments.*

Questions to be discussed in the group

1. What things helped us to "share the work" in a partnership?

2. What were some of the barriers to supporting the partnership concept?

3. What is something I can do differently that would help support or improve our partnership care delivery strategies?

4. What are some ways I can show support to my co-workers?

Discussion/Reflection

Example:

Partners in Practice Discussion Activity

(page 1 of 2)

115

1. Set up several discussion group times to discuss with the staff the situations they recently encountered during care delivering using the partnership model.

2. Begin the session by reviewing the purpose for the discussion group and the relationship guidelines you will use in the discussion (For example, you should go over the Commitment to my Co-worker card.[1])

3. Create an environment that is safe and welcoming for all participants.

4. Review criteria for competency assessment below. (First and foremost, this discussion group is not a test with right or wrong answers. The goal is to create discussion and address ways to improve our relationships and support quality care delivery.)

<u>Measurement for individual competency:</u>

- Everyone must participate by sharing something to complete this competency activity.

- The discussion must include each person articulating a way he or she will support the partnership model and its ongoing improvement. Everyone must state something they will do.

- There's no judge or "check off person" in this process. That is the key to ongoing competency assessment. Then the group will decide (as a group) if they met the overall intent/objective of the discussion.

It is not about having the answer today, but having the courage to keep asking the questions that address the challenges of tomorrow.

Example:

Partners in Practice Discussion Activity

(page 2 of 2)

Charge Nurse Staffing Skills Competency (Psychiatry)

This is one method to meet the Charge Nurse competency. Any unit or individual may help develop a method of assessment as long as it meets the criteria for the competency and is approved by your unit education council.

- -

To Complete the Charge Nurse Skill Worksheet:

- Familiarize yourself with the staffing policy attached.
- Use the worksheet to make staffing assignments for the unit illustrated.

Tips:

- Don't make it more complex than it is. Only use information given, even if it is sketchy.
- In this scenario we have included the use of paraprofessionals (PAs) or assigning patients to the Charge Nurse.

Discussion/Reflection

Example:

Charge Nurse Staffing Discussion Group Tool

(page 1 of 5)

TITLE STAFFING ASSIGNMENTS		MANUAL Policy Manual
AUTHOR:	POSITION:	FILE ALPHABETICALLY WITH SECTION:
APPROVAL BODY: Director's Group	CHAIR:	REVIEW DATE:
		REVISION DATE:

Example:

Charge Nurse Staffing Discussion Group Tool

(page 2 of 5)

POLICY

The Charge Nurse or Nurse Manager is responsible for patient assignment of staff. The following criteria are considered in determining staffing assignments for each shift.

A. Experience and expertise of available staff

   1. Educational preparation

   2. Qualifications of staff

   3. Orientation completed

   4. Role limitation (including clinical practice limitations of Float Pool staff; see Nursing Services policy)

B. Patient classification data

C. Patient care needs/priorities, including patient teaching and discharge planning needs

D. Patient Care Unit care delivery system

E. Infection control parameters

F. Health status or limitations of staff

G. Special interests of staff

H. Availability of support/specialist resources

I. Patient requests

J. Geography of Patient Care Unit

To the extent possible, an RN will make a patient assessment before delegating appropriate aspects of nursing care to ancillary personnel.

Nursing Services staff will be assigned accountability to all patients, even when nursing students are given primary assignments.

REVIEWING AUTHORITY	TITLE	DATE
REVIEWING AUTHORITY	TITLE	DATE
REVIEWING AUTHORITY	TITLE	DATE

Discussion/Reflection

Charge Nurse Skill Worksheet (Psychiatry)

You are charge nurse of this Psych unit. You have 15 patients and a total of 5 staff working for day shift. Use the criteria on staffing polices and information below to make your assignments.

Patients

- Tom—28 yo, Biopolar manic, high activity, irritable
- Molly—32 yo, Depression/ED, observe 1 hr. after meals
- James—40 yo, Depression with SI, placement issues
- Tanya—33yo, Depression with SI, SP, HIV positive
- Debbie—25 yo, Psychotic Decompensation, ADLs
- Joe—55 yo, Dangerous to self, SP, CT scan
- Sam—18 yo, Conduct D/O, sexual prec, dope prec.
- LuAnn—50 yo, Paranoid Schiz. med adjustment, actively hallucinating
- Dick—55 yo, Depression, cooperative/discharge
- Richard—49 yo, Failure outpatient treatment, left arm wound with dressing changes
- Brian—28 yo, danger to self
- David—45 yo, Depression, ECT, confused
- Lynee—65 yo, Para Schiz/Dementia/R/O organic, confused, help with ALL ADLs.
- Kathy—34 yo, Depression, very withdrawn, suicidal
- Wendy—20 yo, Depression, Dissociative D/O
- 1st Admit—unknown

Staff

- Sally—charge nurse
- Sue—Unit staff, 1 yr on unit, 10 years experience, pregnant
- Nancy—Unit staff, 4 yrs experience
- Glinda—RN from float pool
- Larry—Unit Psych assistant (PA) with 2 yrs experience

Also Assign

- Medications to one nurse (8a–12n)
- Roves (each hour) include 15" checks
- Team meeting at 10a and 11a
- Food monitor, breakfast (7:30a) and lunch (12n)
- Goal group, 9 AM
- Support group, 1 PM

Discussion/Reflection

Example:

Charge Nurse Staffing Discussion Group Tool

(page 3 of 5)

Indicate Patient assignments

Sally, RN	Sue, RN	Nancy, RN	Glinda, RN	Larry, PA

Other duties

We, as a group, have discussed and reflected on the assignment-making options for the situation above. We feel, using the criteria and policies presented, that we have come up with one (or more) ways to address the staffing needs in this example.

❑ All members of the discussion group agree.

Signatures of group members _____

_____ _____

_____ _____

❑ I, as the group facilitator, endorse this group decision. Signature of facilitator _____

Note: If you as a group facilitator do not feel the goal of the discussion group was met, that is O.K. Set up a time to try another discussion group in the future. Critical thinking skills and team skills take time to evolve. Allow your group the opportunity to strengthen these skills over time.

Discussion/Reflection

Example:

Charge Nurse
Staffing
Discussion
Group Tool

(page 4 of 5)

Charge Nurse Staffing Skills
Psychiatry Competencey Answers

1. The following patients must be assigned to a nurse:
   Molly, Tanya, Sam, LuAnn, Dick, David, Kathy,
   Wendy

2. Tasks should be shared.
   Med cannot be with **Food**.
   Food cannot be with **Goal**.
   Team cannot be with **Support Group**.

3. **Roves** cannot conflict with other tasks.

4. If the Psych Assistant is assigned patients patients
   directly, those patients need a Registered Nurse
   co-assigned to oversee their care.

Discussion/Reflection

Example:

Charge Nurse
Staffing
Discussion
Group Tool

(page 5 of 5)

Presentations

Presentations can be used to assess competencies that deal with knowledge and understanding.

As many educators know, to teach someone a concept, you must first understand it yourself. Using presentations is a valid way to measure competency of a presenter's knowledge and understanding of a subject.

By using presentations as a verification method, you promote individual mastery of the information while introducing the information to other individuals. This creates an environment in which the sharing of information is valued and rewarded.

Usually individuals are asked to share information they have gained from experience or from a recent educational event (such as a conference). Some individuals, when asked to present, will hesitate, either because they don't feel comfortable carrying out this type of activity, or because it seems too time consuming. If you suggest that this activity can be used to verify a competency, it is often the stimulus people need to do a presentation.

Because not everyone will be able to do a presentation to verify competency on a specific topic, you will need to provide other verification methods for those who do not present. Make sure that the presenter is not also required to complete the other designated competency verification methods.

Note: This verification category refers to *giving* a presentation, not merely attending one. Just attending a class, in-service, or presentation does not provide assessment for competency. For a class or in-service to be used as a measurement for competency assessment, the class must include one of the other verification methods listed in this chapter (for example, test, group discussion, case study, etc.)

IMPORTANT

One of the simplest ways to verify and document a competency of knowledge/understanding through the use of a presentation is as follows:

Example:

Have an individual present his or her knowledge or understanding of a concept, model, method, or idea. After the presentation is over, ask the audience members to fill out a comment card:

After hearing this presentation,

❏ *I feel comfortable putting this/these concepts into daily practice.*

❏ *I do not feel comfortable at this time putting this into my daily practice.*

This is a great way to measure understanding of the concept *by the presenter.* If a presenter does not really understand the concept, it is difficult to explain it to others in a way that would allow them to understand and use it.

Physicians have used presentation as a form of competency verification for more than 100 years. These presentations are often referred to as "case presentations" or "grand rounds." See one example on the next page.

Presentations

Continuing Medical Education Activity

Nov. 5th, 8:30-9:30 am
Medical Center Lecture Hall

Tumor Board Case Studies

Objective: At the conclusion of the activity, the participant will be able to:

1. list diagnostic tests necessary to diagnose cancers based on appropriate history and physical exam.

2. identify the stage of the cancer based on the results of diagnostic study.

3. identify accepted treatment and recognize investigational protocols for various cancer therapies.

4. list and apply ancillary services available for cancer patients using a multi-disciplinary approach.

5. explain modalities available for pain control.

Method: Case Discussion/Lecture Presentation

Presenter: Dr. H. Platteau

Cases to be presented and discussed:

Patients	*Surgical #*	*Diagnoses*
A. G.	S-0907-97	37 y. o. female with skin tumor of the back
H. Z.	S-0916-97	60 y. o. male with neck mass

The Medical Center designates this educational activity for a maximum of one hour in category 1 credit towards the AMA Physician recognition award. Each physician should claim only those hours of credit he or she actually spends in the educational activity.

Presentations

Example:

This is a good example of a use of presentation as a competency verification by Dr. H. Platteau, the presenter.

Mock Events/Surveys

Mock events can be used to assess responses in daily work or practice.

Mock events are simulations of real-world situations. They are carried out either in the work setting or in an artificial laboratory (such as a skills lab). Mock events are educational and assessment activities that can measure the ability of an individual or team to carry out a job function under the time, stress, and reality of a potential work-related situation. This is often used for events that are high-risk, time-dependent, infrequent, or hazardous. Here are a few examples of mock events:

- Mock codes
- Simulated disaster drills or other emergency situations
- Mock surveys for accreditation or inspection agencies
- Mock drills (such as fire, severe weather, power outages, terrorist threats, etc.)
- Hazardous material spill clean-ups
- Mock surveys of proper equipment use and maintenance
- Mock financial audits

WARNING

Mock events reflect individual performance. You cannot conduct a mock event in a work setting with only some employees and conclude that all employees in that area are competent to perform those skills. Only those individuals who participate in the mock event are eligible for verification.

IMPORTANT

Debriefing sessions following a mock event are an essential element. You will get more out of a mock event by reflecting on the actions that were taken during the event. It also helps deal with some of the anxieties the event itself may have produced. Recognizing mistakes and identifying actions take next time are an essential part of ongoing learning and development, so be sure to make debriefing a part of your next mock event.

Debriefing sessions are also very appropriate following real-world disasters and stressful events. The sessions can serve to assess actions taken in the actual event.

Example 1:

Use a debriefing session after your next code to assess the roles carried out by each person and the group communication and problem solving. This can identify whether job functions were carried out in an appropriate manner, or if team behaviors helped or hindered the outcomes.

Example 2:

Spend some time reviewing the steps taken and communication strategies used after your organization has responded to a disaster or severe weather situation. Look for ways to improve performance, as well as to reward effort. Debriefing strategies have been shown to decrease anxieties and increase confidence for future action. Debriefing sessions are considered discussion/ reflection group activities. See pages 111–121 for more information on these types of activities.

Mock events can be planned and announced to the participants ahead of time or they can be done unannounced. Mock events can be in conjunction with an education event or stand alone as merely a verification of skill(s). Mock events are one of the best methods available to measure response in the real world. For example, if you have a cardiopulmonary resuscitation (CPR) card, this card indicates you are certified in basic CPR skills. To obtain this card, you completed a test and did a return demonstration on a CPR mannequin. However, this card does not mean you can actually respond in an emergency. Some people with CPR cards have frozen in their tracks during an emergency and could not carry out the knowledge-based skills and psychomotor skills they know. A mock event is a great way to assess this potential ability to respond.

Mock Events/Surveys

Quality Improvement Monitors

QI monitors can be used to measure any of the three skill domains. Any time a QI monitor reflects individual performance, it is automatically a verification of competency as well.

QI monitors or Performance Improvement (PI) monitors are common tools we use to monitor the environment and the outcomes for our customers. QI monitors are often used to check compliance with policies and protocols as well as to benchmark desired outcomes and the successful achievement of these outcomes.

QI monitors give us valuable information about the progress and performance of the organization. These tools can also be useful in verifying competencies of individuals. Many of the QI tools we use to assess overall organizational performance start by collecting data on individual performance. Here are some examples of where QI monitors may be used for individual performance indicators. You probably already have these monitors in place to measure overall outcomes.

- *Chart/Documentation audits*
- *Compliance with Infection Control policies*
- *Appropriate equipment set-up/teardown/clean-up*

When using QI monitors for competency assessment, remember that the QI monitor must reflect individual performance. You cannot monitor 10% of the group and conclude from the data that the entire group is competent in that area. The monitor must reflect an *individual's* performance.

Because most QI monitors are not designed to capture the performance of every employee, you will need to have more than one way for the group to verify competencies. A QI monitor can be offered as one of the verification methods to assess an identified competency. As mentioned before, giving people more than one option is very valuable. This reflects many of the concepts of adult learning. By allowing individuals to choose their competency verification methods, you increase accountability and show respect for the individuals.

Choosing a competency for which QI monitoring is a competency verification can also have an impact on your QI program. Selecting a QI monitor as a verification method encourages people to be a part of the QI process. It may even be the impetus that gets some people involved in QI who never were

Quality Improvement

before. Using QI monitors as a competency verification tool can benefit both your competency assessment process and your quality improvement process.

Example:

Here is one example of how an organization used a QI monitor to assess skills in the documentation of patient education.

This organization's leadership had a great deal of QI data showing that they were not documenting patient education. They created a competency around this issue and decided to use their QI monitoring process as a method to verify this identified competency.

They modified their Patient Education Documentation QI monitor to reflect not only that documentation was done correctly, but who did it. Making this change in the QI monitor allowed the data to reflect individual performance and skill. Then each staff member was asked to use the QI data to demonstrate that he or she successfully completed patient education each quarter. This required the employee to go to the QI log book and look for his or her name each quarter.

A few benefits from this process were that:

- Employees became familiar with the QI log book.
- Employees realized that they needed to document patient education in order for it to be captured in the QI data, so they started to do more accurate documentation.
- Seeing other colleagues in the QI log book accomplishing successful documentation tended to create good-natured competition, inspiring others to do better documentation themselves.

Overall, this competency approach helped this organization improve individual skills associated with patient education documentation, while providing a few other benefits along the way.

Quality Improvement

Universal Blood and Body Substances Techniques Observation
Quality Improvement Data Collection Form

Key	
+	Met Indicator
−	Did not Meet Indicator
NA	Not Applicable

Work Area _____ Data Collector _____ Employee _____

Guidelines for data retrieval: Observe staff during procedure in every day practice. Score a positive for a technique that is in compliance with the indicator. Score a negative if not in compliance.

Indicators	+	−	NA	expected	Remarks
1. Employee wore gloves to touch any body substance (blood, stool, drainage, etc.).				100%	
2. Employee wore gloves to touch any item, bed clothes, or skin soiled with body substances.				100%	
3. Employee wore gloves to touch non-intact skin of patient and/or protect his or her own non-intact skin.				100%	
4. Employee wore a gown when he or she anticipated clothing might become soiled with body substances.				100%	
5. Employee wore a mask during any procedure in which he or she anticipated body substance might splash or spray.				100%	
6. Employee wore protective eyewear during any procedure in which he or she anticipated body substance might splash or spray. (Personal glasses need solid side shields, permanently affixed.)				100%	
7. Employees washed their hands after removing gloves.				100%	
8. Employee discarded needles and other sharp instruments in a puncture-resistant container.				100%	
9. Employee did not recap dirty needles.					

Quality Improvement

Example:

QI Data
Collection
Form

Summary of Competency Verification Methods

This chapter discussed the 11 categories of competency verification. There is no *single* method that can capture all the domains of skills—technical, critical thinking and interpersonal. Therefore, you will need to use a combination of methods to create a sound competency assessment program. One of the keys to this success is to match the right competency verification methods to the right competency. Do not just create a form or checklist and then put every competency you have on this checklist. This is the most common mistake organizations make. Take the time to select the appropriate verification methods and to offer a variety of options from the 11 categories in your overall competency assessment process. You will be pleased with the improvement in your overall competency process outcomes if you use this approach.

IMPORTANT Remember that when articulating which verification method will be available as a choice for each competency, you should be specific. Do not just indicate general competency verification methods; actually indicate a specific verification tool to be used.

Always identify exactly what specific verification methods from which employees may choose. On the following page are some examples of how you might present the various options to your employees. Note that the verification methods are selected for their effectiveness in assessing the exact skill or skills they're selected to assess. They also refer to a specific document, tool or activity in detail.

Right

Competency Statement	Verification Methods
Demonstrates the ability to apply customer service principals to everyday work situations.	❏ Submit two Customer Services Peer Reviews completed by two different coworkers. (See p. 100) ❏ Submit one Customer Service Exemplar based on information from a patient/family member (See p. 89–90). Include cards, letters, or patient satisfaction information that identifies you by name. ❏ Submit one Building Bridges Exemplar (See p. 91) ❏ Participate in one of the Customer Service case study/discussions group sessions. (See Newsletter for date and location Pre-registration is required. A prep packet will be sent to you prior to the session.)

Offering a variety of verification categories give employees choices, which shows respect for them as adult learners and gives them the opportunity to buy into the assessment process. This verification sampling is excellent.

What follows, however, is an example of a verification sampling that would be more likely to create confusion than enthusiasm in the people to whom it is directed.

Wrong

Competency Statement	Verification Methods
Demonstrates the ability to apply customer service principals to everyday situations.	❑ Peer review ❑ Exemplar ❑ Case Study/Discussion Group

This approach is too vague, and can lead to misunderstandings. It also requires a greater level of follow-up communication on the part of the educator or manager, and it may lead to "spoon-feeding" the employee further information, or having to correct employee actions when they misinterpret the verification method choices. This can create a lack of credibility and accountability in the process.

Another approach to avoid is that of creating a general competency verification grid on your competency form, like the one that follows.

Competency Statement	Method of Verification	Assessed by...	Date
Competency #1			
Competency #2			
Competency #3			
Verification Method Codes:			

Verification Method Codes:

RD= Return Demonstration	E= Exemplar
T= Test	CS= Case Study
V= Verbalized	P= Peer Review

This approach is not only vague, but it also leaves the matching of a verification method to the competency up to an assessor or the employee. Neither may have the expertise to select the appropriate matches. This selection is often best done by an educator or staff development specialist.

And once again, when creating your competency form, be careful not to call your competency form a "checklist." This implies that all of your competencies will be measured by return demonstration (the category under which checklists fall).

Also be careful not to *design* your competency form in the format of a return demonstration (or check-off form).

Here is an example of this format that should be avoided:

Competency Statement	Verification		Date	Assessed by...
	Met	Not Met		
Competency #1				
Competency #2				
Competency #3				
Competency #4				
Competency #5				
Competency #6				

By designing your competency form like this, you create only one method of verification for all your competencies. This form requires observation by an assessor, so this form requires a return demonstration of some kind for every competency listed. As mentioned earlier in this chapter, there is no single verification method that can measure all of your competencies. It is essential to use a combination of verification methods in your competency assessment.

Notes

chapter five

Secrets of a Successful Competency Process

- Incorporating competency assessment into daily practice

- Packaging and communicating the competency process

- Managers' responses to competency problems and deficits

- Tracking and documenting the competency process

- Incorporating age-specific, cultural, and safety aspects of competency assessment

Incorporating Competency Assessment into Daily Operations

In order to create a truly successful competency process, it is important to incorporate quality improvement (QI) activities into the overall assessment process. *Quality Improvement is defined as any system that brings a problem to the surface and directs it to someone who can do something about it.*

To incorporate QI into the competency process, start with your vision. With every effort your organization pursues, ask "What are we trying to achieve?" As you begin a new initiative or change, start with education. Allow for some implementation and application time. Then use a QI monitor to assess the progress of the initiative or change. The results from QI data will indicate whether implementation was successful. If the data indicates a problem, you can at that point develop a competency that reflects this need.

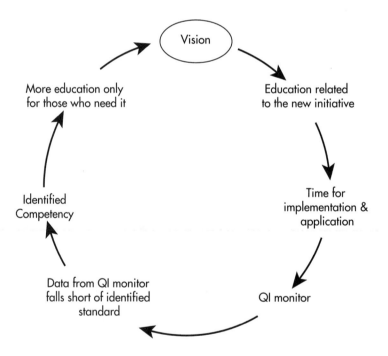

By following these steps to incorporating competency into daily operation, we create a sound, functional system. Competency assessment is never the first step. If we articulate the vision and provide support for its success, and then monitor our progress through QI, we can actually save time and money. The QI data may already measure competency in a certain skill; further competency assessment may unnecessary.

This approach is not only cost effective, but it also streamlines competency assessment by keeping the focus on the skills actually needed in a given situation. For example, it may not be a lack of a technical skill (such as following a procedure) that is preventing employees from achieving a desired outcome. It may be lack of an attitudinal skill (such as consistently applying the skills they have in all situations).

Example:

The skill of handwashing is a perfect example.

It is not that employees do not know how to wash their hands; the problem is that they do not have the attitude or mind-set to apply that skill all day every day. If you approach handwashing with a competency first, rather than with QI, you would probably focus on developing a technical skill competency. If you do the QI first, you would uncover the real problem. The problem is not a lack of technical skill, but a lack of attitudinal skill.

Competency Assessment focuses on verification, not education.

Sometimes one QI monitor is not enough. If you find that outcomes from a QI monitor fall below expectations, it may be wise to conduct a second, more detailed, QI monitor to really identify the root cause of the problem you're experiencing. This is illustrated in the previous handwashing example. With results from only one level of QI, it is very easy to jump to the conclusion that you need to do handwashing inservices. But in reality, this is rarely the solution.

It would be better to use a QI process to determine who, if anyone, is washing their hands at the standard expected and then to compare groups producing acceptable handwashing outcomes with groups producing unacceptable outcomes. Then you can uncover the real issues getting in the way of success.

On one occasion when I ran into this situation, we conducted a second QI around those who were achieving successful outcomes. We found the difference between the successful and unsuccessful groups was the successful group's ability to creatively monitor each other and openly communicate in a way that motivated people to remain consistent in their practice. Through the second level of QI, we discovered that there was no lack of skill in handwashing itself, but there was a lack of skill in carrying out individual enforcement of the practice through creative communication strategies. We then put our energy into building these creative communication skills and later found through QI monitors that handwashing began to improve.

After the competency is identified, focus on the skill required, not the education. Only use education for those individuals who need it—those who are having difficulty achieving and verifying the identified competency. This is a much more cost-effective approach.

Malcolm Knowles (1970) stated, "A learning need is the gap between the learner's present level of competence and a higher level of performance which is defined by the learner, the organization or society." Learning or education is not the required element—the competency expectation or *verification* is the required element. If people have the skill already, then education is not required. Education is for only those who do not have the skill already.

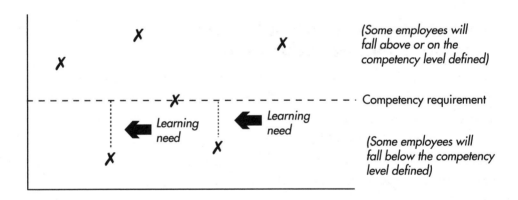

Keeping Control of Competency Identification

As mentioned earlier, each group (unit, area, department) should sit down each competency period, and use the worksheet on p.25 to identify their competencies for the year. People have found this to be a very successful approach. Sometimes this approach has been so successful that groups begin to realize competencies are a way to draw attention to issues and stimulate change. A problem can develop, however, when people in other departments and areas start to suggest competencies to other departments and areas.

Example:

Pharmacy sees problems with medication errors, and tells nursing they need to do a medication competency. Then nursing tells pharmacy, "Well, then you need a competency on @$!*?#!"

Do not let any group give any *other* group a competency.

WARNING

In a successful competency process, the unit or group itself is the only place where competencies can be identified and prioritized for that group. No other individual or group should force a competency on them. Another group can share data and outcome findings with them, but the group itself will ultimately be the final decision maker in the competency selection for its area.

In the same way, committees and task forces formed by the organization can go crazy creating organization-wide competencies. It is very easy for a committee, in their efforts to deal with a problem or sentinel event, to use a house-wide competency as an intervention. When committee after committee throughout the organization does this, one individual can end up needing to complete 20, 30, 40 or more competencies. As you may recall from chapter 2, we are trying to keep the number to 10 or fewer. This means 10 or fewer *total*—one set of 10 or fewer competencies reflecting *all* of the competency needs at the unit/area, department, organization, (and corporate, if applicable) levels.

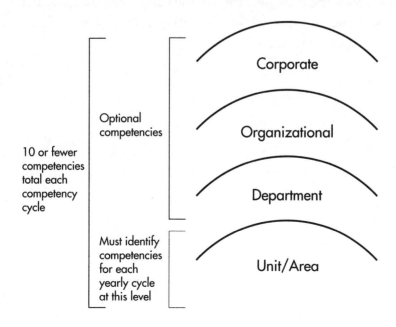

If you choose to have some department, organization or corporate competencies, that is okay, but choose one or two only. Keep in mind that the focus of the competency process, and the source of its success, is to keep the control of the competency efforts as close to the patients and customers as possible. This means as much control as possible should be given to the staff and units/departments delivering service every day. To control and dictate too many competencies from the top down can be disastrous. Be very careful. Any identified departmental, organizational, or corporate competency should be reviewed within the overall competency goals. Do not just put out organizational competencies in response to an issue; scrutinize the effect this organizational competency will have on the organization and the overall competency goals.

I recommend all departmental, organizational, and corporate competencies go through a competency committee (or some organized group) for approval. This is a great way to stop competencies from getting out of control.

Packaging and Communicating the Competency Assessment Process

Putting forth a clear picture of the competency process, along with your expectations for it, is essential for competency assessment success. The following communication tool regarding competency process is an example of how to package and communicate the beginning steps of the competency process. This communication can be sent out to the leadership of each area responsible for overseeing competency assessment.

Developing Competencies for Your Area

Step 1:

Identify the job classes in your area. Determine whether you will need initial or ongoing competencies for each job class. (See algorithm page 142)

Step 2:

Gather the supervisor and at least two representatives of the job class to help identify possible competencies. Use the Ongoing Competency Worksheet to assist in the identification of ongoing competencies, and the guidelines on page 27–29 to help with initial competencies development.

Step 3:

Develop competencies statements from prioritized lists on worksheet. These statements should reflect the outcome you expect from 100% of staff in that job class. Competencies should be concise and measurable.

Step 4:

Develop verification methods that reflect successful achievement of the competency statement.

Step 5:

Print the competencies and verification methods for each job class on the attached competency assessment form (see page 38). The organizational competencies are already printed on the form. You will need a separate form for each job class. Copy this form and distribute one to each employee. Send one copy to the Education Department for archiving.

Step 6:

Each employee is responsible to verify his or her competencies. Each supervisor is responsible for creating an environment that promotes competency assessment. Clearly communicate the timeline for competency assessment, as well as ways to achieve competency verification (i.e. make verification part of staff meetings and other work area activities.).

Who Does Which Competencies?

We have talked about initial competencies and ongoing competencies. What happens if you hire someone half way through a competency year? Do they complete both initial and ongoing competencies? When do they start the next set of competencies? A quick answer to these questions is found in the competency algorithm below.

In short, a person only does one set of competencies in a year (or a given competency cycle). So you either do initial competencies *or* ongoing competencies but never both in the same year.

Competency Algorithm

100% of all your staff need to be assessed each competency cycle. They will either complete initial *or* ongoing competencies.

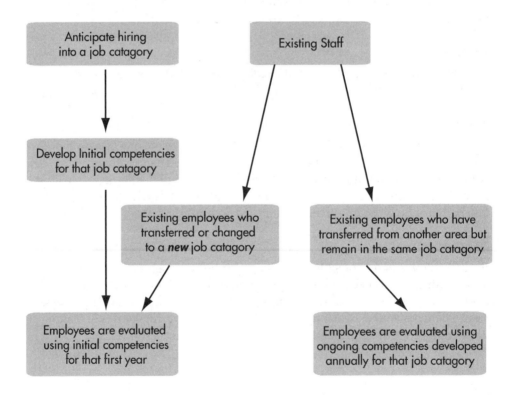

Let's say you do your ongoing competency cycle from January to December. You hire a new employee in March. The initial competency period for that job is three months. The new employee must complete his or her initial competencies by June. Then they do not have any more competencies until January of the following year when they join the team in the next competency cycle.

Or maybe you have an employee who transfers from one area to another but is basically in the same job category. They would not have to finish the competencies from their last area because they are no longer working in the area. Instead, they would be expected to complete the ongoing competencies in the new area. Deadlines and time frames should be considered if an employee transfers late into the competency year.

If the employee is transferred to a new area and is *changing* his or her job category, that employee also does not need to finish the ongoing competencies in the last area, but instead starts the initial competency requirements for the new area.

This means any employee will only do *one* set of competencies in a given cycle.

Communicating Competencies to the Staff

Once the competencies for a given time period have been identified, they need to be communicated to the people that need to complete them. An explanation of the competencies and the competency process should be included in this communication. When creating this communication, keep in mind these are some of the questions and objections that may be floating in your employees' minds. These actual statements heard from employees may be helpful:

- Why do I need to prove I am competent after 20 years of experience?
- What happens if I am not found competent?
- Why do we have to do this?
- Is this a way for the organization to get rid of dead wood?
- Don't you know if I am competent by now?!
- What will you gain by this?

Do not overlook the importance of this communication. Explaining the process and its purpose ahead of time helps create understanding and buy-in. When competency expectations and the competency process are clearly communicated, you can create wonderful things. Here are some staff responses at the end of their first competency cycle using the approaches illustrated throughout this book.

Staff Quotes Regarding Competency

- Competency raised our critical thinking skills.
- The emphasis was on individual accountability.

- This is the beginning of a movement to make staff accountable and responsible for their professional education and practice.
- This helped us and encouraged us to evaluate important knowledge, skills and abilities in our practice.
- We worked as a group on common goals.
- This is a reaffirmation of what we know we can do.
- The competency process helped us point out areas of discrepancy in our work.

Essential Elements of Successful Organizational Operations

There are five basic elements required to make any organization's daily operations successful. These elements are vision, leadership communication, competency assessment, quality improvement, and leadership response. If any of these elements is overlooked, the organization will struggle for success.

The Essential Elements to Successful Organizational Operations

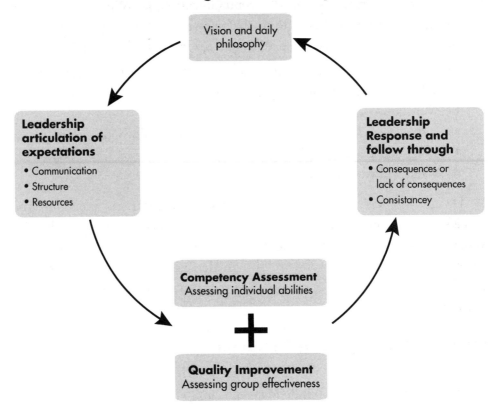

Let's examine these elements:

Vision or daily philosophy refers to anything that sets the general goals and direction for the organization. It can be a mission statement, a policy, a memo that is posted on the bulletin board, or an informal rule the group has created. It is the shared goal or philosophy that is lived by in daily actions.

Leadership then articulates the vision. This is done through communication, structure, and resources. Leaders do this through memos and staff meetings, as well as informal verbal communication and gestures. Leadership also articulates the vision through the structure of the organization and allocation of resources. For example, if we wanted people to use more computers at work, we could verbalize this expectation to employees at meetings and through memos. However, if we did not buy them any computers, they wouldn't take our messages very seriously because we are not willing to put resources behind our vision. Leaders "articulate" their vision many different ways.

The next step is to stop and look at ourselves as a group. We do this through **competency assessment** and **quality improvement** efforts. We stop periodically and "take a snapshot" of who we are and how we are doing. We check individuals' current level of skill, and we examine team effectiveness and outcomes through quality improvement and performance improvement efforts. These assessments and measures give us a picture of how we are doing.

After we have a picture of how the group is doing, **we respond as leaders.** We respond with consequences or a lack of consequences, consistency or a lack of consistency. Even "no response" is a response of some kind. This step in the Essential Elements Model is the most important because it directly impacts vision and daily philosophy. Whatever our leadership response is, we either create a new vision or reinforce the current one. You cannot re-write a policy or mission statement to change the reality you have created through you actions. It is powerful. So if we spoon-feed people, after we have asked them to do something, they will come to expect that you will rescue them, regardless of how many times you re-write the policy or expectation. You actions speak louder than words.

Most organizations struggle with this last element of leadership response. We need to ask if our leaders have the skills or competencies to carry out this element in our organizations, and whether they get the support they need when they do. This is the number one competency deficit found in most organizations. Our leaders do not know how to be creative with consequences or to keep their efforts consistent. They need our help and support in this matter.

The Manager's Response and Follow-up to Competency Assessment Issues

Managers set the tone and create an environment that supports individual accountability for competency assessment. The manager's response to the competency process will establish the overall philosophy of the competency program for the future. Policies will not create support for the competency process. Leadership actions will.

Articulating Competency Expectations

Leaders and managers will articulate the expectations of the competency process through their communication, through structures that are established to support competency assessment, and through what resources they dedicate to the process. Employees cannot successfully complete the competency process unless they clearly understand what's expected of them. We need to help managers develop creative ways to articulate the competency process to all employees. This includes articulation of the employee's accountability in the competency process. Managers should not complete the competency assessment process for the employee. Instead managers should clearly define the process and how the employees can meet the competency assessment requirements.

Establishing Consequences

The most critical elements to the success of a competency assessment process are the consequences and follow-up demonstrated by managers when employees do not successfully complete the process. The consequences (or lack of consequences) will determine the ultimate effectiveness of your competency program.

When I talk to leaders, many are surprised that their employees do not take the process seriously, or that they do not accept accountability. I usually ask, "What happens if they don't do their competencies?" If the answer is, "Nothing," then I am not surprised if their program is unsuccessful. In situations like these, the leaders themselves are not taking the process seriously.

Most employees will complete the competency requirements that have been asked of them. But there will *always* be one or two people who do not. If leaders do not take some action with these employees, the other employees will begin to say "why should we try?"

Defining Consequences

Creating an action plan or consequences for an employee who has fallen below the expected minimum standard is never easy. Most of us struggle with even identifying consequences.

Most leaders can think of only one consequence for individuals who do not successfully complete their competencies: fire them. But there are so many more choices than that. Because there are many different situations and people respond in many different ways to the competency process, managers need many different responses.

One of the best ways to come up with a variety of approaches to employee behavior is to discuss options with other managers. By sharing possible situations with peers, you can collect a variety of possible consequences. Also ask yourself what motivates you to do your work or to take responsible action. Consequences can be positive or negative. Creative consequences may be more obvious than you think.

Consequences should be put into place long before competencies are due. I like to have consequences that motivate positive behavior in the competencies process. I also like to have consequences occur throughout the year, not just at the end of the year.

Example:

As I mentioned before, it is beneficial to give employees a variety of options to validate their competencies. For example, for one of your selected competencies for the year, you could offer 4 verification method choices—things such as a skills fair (with door prizes and games), a case study discussion group, a self-learning packet with case studies in it, and reading a policy and taking a test. Set up these four verification method choices so that throughout the year the fun choices start to disappear as the year goes on. By the end of the year, you should only have one or two choices left—and they will always be the ones that are "no fun to do." If employees wait until the end of the year to finally do their competency then the only choice they may have left is something that is not so fun to do—something dry like reading the policy and taking the test.

This approach sends the message that if you get motivated early, you will have more fun than if you wait until the last minute. This becomes a consequence—one that rewards positive behavior and discourages negative behavior.

Holding Managers and Leaders Accountable

We often discuss the issue of staff taking accountability. We all know that this issue is also true for our managers and leaders. Many times, as an organization gets ready to implement a change, some of the managers do not follow through on their given assignments.

Example:

> Let's say you are implementing a new competency assessment approach. You ask each manager in each department to begin identifying competencies in their areas by using the ongoing competency worksheet. Most of the managers do it, but…there is always one or two who do not. What do you do?

Again, there must be consequences. But how do you do that with managers? And what if the problem is further up the organizational ladder?

Here is an example of possible consequence:

> Most of us are motivated by "Wanting to look good in front of others." The worksheet on the following page shows a tool used in an organization to track progress of manager involvement and support in a competency process change. By distributing this tracking tool periodically at management meetings to communicate the progress of the implementation, they created a situation where people either look good (or not so good) in front of their colleagues. Thereby establishing a consequence for the managers involved before the end of the implementation period.

Departmental Progress of Competence Assessment Implementation

Department	Director/ Manager	Intro to Concept[1]	*Work Started[2]	Process in place[3]
Administration	Richard Wayne	☐	☐	☐
Admissions & Outpatient Registration	Beth Chase	☐	☐	☐
Ambulatory Care Services	DeAnn Renate	■	■	■
Attorney's Office	Max Vankerckhove	☐	☐	☐
Bone Marrow Transplant Program	Janet Pearson	☐	☐	☐
Cardiovascular Services	Beth Michaels	■	■	■
Center for Spiritual Care and Healing	Adrien Alexander	■	■	☐
Children's Services	Claudia Burrer	■	☐	☐
Diagnostic Radiology	Jean Mauricette	☐	☐	☐
Educational Services	Donna Kellogg	■	■	■
Emergency Department	Veronica Beaty	■	■	■
Endoscopy	Mike Emanuel	■	■	■
Engineering/Maintenance and Operations	Ronald Branislav	■	☐	☐
Environmental Services	Pauline Gilbert	■	☐	☐
Financial Accounting	Paul Henris	☐	☐	☐
Hemophilia Center	Darlene Mathias	■	■	■
Home Health Care Services	Ramona Mehlhoff	Scheduled	☐	☐

Example:

This is a great way to track and motivate manager involvement in your competency process.

(page 1 of 3)

Departmental Progress of Competence Assessment Implementation

Department	Director/Manager	Intro to Concept[1]	*Work Started[2]	Process in place[3]
Human Resources	Audrey Bertrand	☐	☐	☐
Information Systems	Chris Bjork	■	■	■
Laboratories	Isabelle Daniels	■	■	☐
Marketing Services	Matthew Richards	Scheduled	☐	☐
Materials and Outreach	Cathy Rolansky	☐	☐	☐
Medical Staff Office	Renee deAnnotelli	☐	☐	☐
Nursing Services	Marilyn Brockel	■	■	■
Administration	Mary Kameron	■	■	■
Pediatric ICU	Brenda Czmowski	■	■	■
Neonatal ICU	Jayne Fahrni	■	■	■
Cath Lab	Shirley Reuer	■	■	■
Pediatrics	Janel Saunders	■	■	■
Cardiology	Leah Keller	■	■	■
Med/Surg	Janeen Beckstrom	■	■	■
Oncology	Susan Edwards-Wesley	■	■	■
Adult Psych	Marie Schuber	■	■	■
Pediatric Support	Dwayne Schwartzkopf	■	■	■

Example:

Manager involvement in competency process.

(page 2 of 3)

Departmental Progress of Competence Assessment Implementation

Department	Manager	Intro to Concept[1]	*Work Started[2]	Process in place[3]
Resources/Float Pool	Colleen Dockter	■	■	■
Same Day Surgery	Lydia Schmidt	■	■	■
Child Family Life	Diane Bergh	■	■	■
Professional Services	Maggie Heyne	■	■	■
Nutrition Services	Deb Dumdie	■	■	■
Patient Accounting Services	Bea Stankovsky	■	■	☐
Patient Relations	Sue Welliver	☐	☐	☐
Perioperative Services	Becky Roberts	Scheduled	☐	☐
Pharmaceutical Services	Dominique Pascale	☐	☐	☐
Protection Services	Tracey Maassen	■	■	■
Quality Support Services	Jason Szymonski	■	■	■
Rehabilitation Services	Michelle Laurence	■	■	■
Social Work	Jill Amundson	■	■	■
Therapeutic Radiology	Vivian Milbertson	■	■	■
Third Party Reimbursement	Emmiline Marino	■	■	■
Transplant Center	Cynthia Forsman	■	■	■
Volunteer Services	Sarah Anderson	■	■	■

[1] Attended the competency workshop, watched the competency videos or checked out prep materials.
[2] Work group formed, employee education started or competency statements drafted.
[3] Competencies identified and sent to Education Services for archiving.

Example:

Manager involvement in competency process.

(page 3 of 3)

Tracking and Documenting

Completion of Competency Assessment

As the manager verifies competency achievement for each individual, some type of competency assessment summary should be sent to a central location (i.e., Human Resources, Education Department, etc.) for overall organizational documentation and tracking. This does not need to be the original individual competency assessment tool. The original competency assessment tools and documents should be kept wherever they are most useful to the employee and manager and only as long as the manager and employee need them to verify competency assessment and support any plan for improvement. After that, they can be discarded.

The minimum that should be kept and archived at a central location is:

- a summary of employees who were deemed competent or not yet competent,
- the action plans associated with those areas that fell short of expectations,
- one original copy of the competencies selected for each area each competency period and examples of the verification methods given as options for the employee to select. (These original competency documents can be paper copies or electronic documents.)

The organization can use tabulation forms or data received from managers to track overall organizational progress and trends that may arise. Some examples of these summary forms are found on the next few pages. Reports of these activities should then be given to executives, your governing body (board of directors, trustees, and so on) and any other key leaders accountable for monitoring organizational progress.

Tracking competency assessment trends in the organization is an essential element to the successful growth of the organization. Collecting and reviewing trends of the aggregate data is required by many regulatory groups (such as Joint Commission). The analysis of trends is also essential for organizational survival and strategic planning; it makes good business sense.

Supervisor Summary of
Employee Competency Completion

Supervisor _____ Dept./Work Area _____

Please indicate the competency status and the date completed (or reviewed) for all the employees you supervise.

Competency Status:

COMP = All competencies successfully validated

NYDC = Not Yet Deemed Competent

NYDC can be used for employees who...

- are on leave
- have not successfully verified all their competencies
- fail to turn in completed competency forms

An action plan must be identified for each employee given an NYDC status.

Please send a copy of each action plan to Human Resources

Employee	Date Completed	Competency Status

Return to Human Resources _____ by _____

Supervisor Evaluation of the Overall Competency Completion

We would like to track issues and trends related to competency assessment. As you compile information regarding each of you employees, please note the following.

What difficulties did employees have in successfully completing competencies?

What worked well in the competency?

Was there any competency that was difficult for the employees to achieve?

Were there any issues relating to the communication of the competency process?

Was competency support available to you and your staff when you needed it?

Please return to _____ by_____.

Thank you!

Location of Competency Documentation

A common question in the competency process is "where do we keep the completed competency data on each employee?" There is *not* one official place for this data to be kept, but your completed competency data must meet three distinct needs:

1) **Competency data must be accessible to managers** to support any ongoing development an employee may need after the competency assessment. Therefore, a manager should have an active file in his or her office with competency data for any employee who has a follow up action plan.

2) **Competency data needs to be collected at some central location** within the organization (Human Resources, Education Department, etc.) This data should be aggregated to identify organizational treads and issues.

3) **Competency data needs to be shared with assignment makers.** Shift supervisors, team leaders and charge nurses need to be aware of competency–based information that will impact workload assignments. This does not mean they will have access to the entire employee file. It simply means a system needs to be established to communicate competency assessment related information to these assignment makers.

Any decisions you make regarding filing of competency documents and data should address these three areas of concern.

Aggregating Data Throughout the Year

There will be several times throughout the year when the competency process will provide useful data. The first time will be when each area is identifying its ongoing competencies for the year (or whatever assessment time period the organization has selected).

Once each area has identified and prioritized which competencies they will do for a given time period, they should send a copy of these competencies to the central location for archiving. By collecting the ongoing competencies selected for a time period, you are creating an excellent "needs assessment" of the whole organization. As you review the competency lists submitted to the central location, look for common themes across departments, such as issues in team communications, customer service, dealing with changes, etc.

Example:

After collecting and reviewing the ongoing competency lists submitted for archiving, you find that 37% of the areas in your organization has some kind of "conflict management" competency. You then would include in your education or staff development strategic plan and budget things that support growth in the area of conflict management. You can offer classes, write newsletter articles on the subject, create posters, buy videos, etc.

So the first opportunity for aggregating data is at the beginning of the competency cycle.

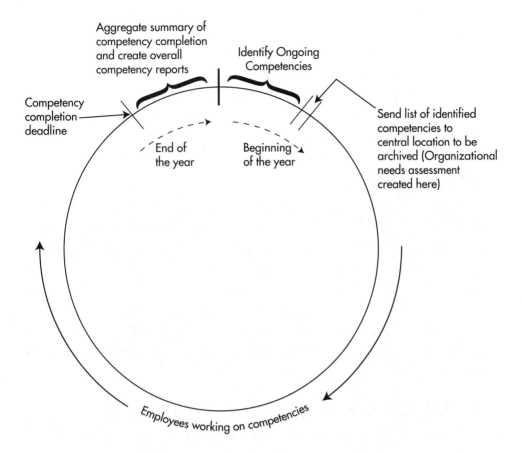

At the end of the competency cycle, there is another opportunity to aggregate data. Set a deadline for competency completion and communicate this clearly to the employees. When the completion deadline arrives, the manager can tabulate the completion of competency assessment for all their employees. Keep in mind that the goal at this point is to document competency assessment of 100% of your staff. Not all the staff may, at this time, be deemed competent (which means they may not have completed all their competency yet). If an employee has 9 out of 10 competencies done, then at the deadline, you document their competency assessment as "Not yet deemed competent" and put an action plan in place that addresses this issue.

So at the completion deadline of each ongoing competency cycle, 100% of your staff can be assessed for competency, but not necessarily will 100% be deemed competent at this time. I would really never expect that you would ever have 100% competent, as you will probably always have at least one employee on a leave of absence. Are they deemed competent for that time period? If they are not there, they did not complete their competencies. And that is okay. At the end of the competency cycle (at the deadline), indicate that they are "Not yet deemed competent," and in the action plan for this person, indicate: "On maternity leave—competency will be expected to be competed upon employee return." This employee has been assessed, but not yet deemed competent, and an appropriate action plan is in place to respond to a situation that deviates from employee expectations articulated to all the staff.

Action Plans

Action plans need to be created for employees who do not meet competency deadlines or expectations. Never extend an overall organizational deadline to meet the needs of one or two individuals who failed to complete things on time. This is too dangerous for your overall competency credibility. Even if the reason for the failure of the employee to complete their competencies is legitimate...DO NOT extend the overall deadline. Instead assess the employee as "not yet deemed competent." Then create an individualized action plan for that employee. You may include in the action plan extra days given to complete their competency or not.

How Do You Create an Action Plan?

First of all you will never be able to write one plan or response that will meet all of the competency issues you will see at the end of each competency cycle. Create a plan that reflects the nature of each employee situation. Some organizations try to write one policy to meet all their needs. It does not work. Some policies say, "If you have not completed your competencies on the deadline, you have an extra 30 days to complete them." In my opinion, that is just "game playing." After awhile, everyone will know the first deadline means nothing. You have really only created a second deadline with this policy

Be prepared. Have a variety of action plans for the variety of competency issues that may arise. You do not need to write piles of policies to carry this out, just a few guiding principles to keep your actions plans consistent as a leadership team.

Here are some things to keep in mind when creating actions plans:

- An action plan should always be of a shorter time frame than the next competency cycle.

  If your competency assessment is done on a yearly basis, then you should never write in an action plan "Not yet deemed competent. Will assess again in one year." Your time frame should be less than a year. You can write "..will assess again in 1 week, 1 month, 6 months," depending on the situation and safety issues involved for your clients and organization.

- When writing your action plan, always include two aspects: how the plan supports the employee and how the plan supports the organizational objectives.

  - Support to the employee includes things like: providing education, one-on-one support, time to develop, providing a clear articulation of the expectations, etc.

  - Support to the organizational objectives include things like: removing the employee from the work area during the development period if they pose a safety hazard to the clients, adjusting work load assignments to reflect current competency levels, or reassignment to another area of service until competency levels are met.

- When creating an action plan, take the time to determine if the employee is going "parallel" with the organization or not (see chapter 1 for details).

- If an employee is going parallel with the organization, they have usually shown some kind of commitment to the organizational expectations.

  ### Example:

  If they cannot make a competency deadline, they come to the manager a month or two before the deadline and ask for help. With this employee I may include in the action plan an extension of the deadline. They are showing commitment to the organization; they just need a little more help or support to be successful.

If an employee is not going parallel with the organization, they usually are not showing commitment to the organizational goals.

Example:

The employee comes to the manager at the end of the competency cycle (the deadline) and says they could not get their competencies done this year. The first question the manager should ask is "Why didn't you tell me this earlier?" If the manager has been telling all the employees throughout the year: "If you are having any problems completing your competencies, stop by my office or give me a call," and the employee had not done so, they have shown a lack of commitment to the overall goals. Please do not spend time, money or energy with educational activities to help develop this employee related to the competencies, instead write up an action plan that addresses the commitment issues. This is a commitment issue, NOT an educational issue.

Age-Specific, Cultural, Safety and Other Aspects of Competency Assessment

Many regulatory standards have helped create awareness for age-specific, cultural and safety aspects of our work. Incorporating these aspects into our competency assessment process is essential to our overall success in achieving our goals. This does not, however, mean that we have to have an age-specific competency every year, or a cultural competency or diversity training yearly. Although such actions may comply with some regulatory standards, this approach can also send a message to your employees that your competency program is based on satisfying regulatory standards instead of on meeting the needs of your organization. Overall, this approach works against building a meaningful philosophy for competency assessment.

We need to integrate age, culture and safety into our competency assessment process. There are many creative ways to do that.

Many skills and abilities are necessary for us to successfully meet our customers' needs. Understanding the age-specific, culture and safety aspects of our customers is essential for us to apply our skills to meet our customers' varied needs. This section will address some of the ways to think about assessing these aspects of skill in your competency program without making it an overwhelming part of the process.

First, you *should* assess age-specific, cultural, safety aspects of your competency assessment program, but that does not mean you must have a separate age-specific competency each year. No regulatory standards require your organization to show an age-specific video every year, or complete age-specific checklists on each employee. Although such actions may comply with some regulatory standards, this approach also can send a message to your employees that your competency program is based on satisfying regulatory standards, and not on meeting the needs of your organization. Overall, this approach works against building a meaningful philosophy for competency assessment.

When identifying the competencies for each job class, do not automatically create an age-specific competency each assessment period. Select the competencies you will require each period based on the Worksheet for Identifying Ongoing Competencies in chapter 2. This worksheet identifies competencies based on what's "new, changing, high-risk, and problematic." Develop a separate age-specific competency only if it comes up as an item when you complete the worksheet.

As stated, assessing age-specific aspects does not mean you have to have a free-standing age-specific competency. Instead it is easier and more meaningful to include age-specific items in the other competencies you identify through the competency worksheet.

Example:

Through the competency worksheet, your group identifies a new customer population you are starting to care for—diabetics. Your group develops a case study to measure the skills and knowledge that the staff should have to treat insulin reactions. The case study describes a 37-year-old patient who is experiencing many symptoms. Questions in the case study ask about the staff's response to her symptoms. The last question asks, "Would you do anything different if this was an 87-year-old woman?" (See page 70 for a sample of this diabetes case study with an age-specific twist.)

You have now included age-specific aspects into your already identified competencies. This approach can often be more realistic and meaningful for staff and better for your overall competency program.

A stand-alone, age-specific competency can be great during orientation when you are first introducing employees to the needs of their customers, but repetition of such competencies can become monotonous and meaningless over time. The best approach is to add the age-specific aspect to other competency needs identified each competency period.

WARNING Never create a competency just to comply with a regulatory standard. This approach is too destructive to your overall program, and has never motivated staff to increase their participation or ownership in the competency process.

As you create any competency, make it meaningful and applicable to the group that is required to complete it. This means that you should avoid "one size fits all" competencies.

Example:

It makes little sense to have the environmental services workers watch an age-specific video describing how toddlers learn and then take a test to measure their skills on age. This may provide an accurate measurement, but it will probably not mean much to the environmental service workers. They may ask, "How does knowing 'how toddlers learn best' help me do my job?"

A better approach:

As part of a recent staff meeting for environmental services, we included on the agenda an opportunity to review the recent changes in cleaning products for the year. We identified that we would be going over the hazardous material information for these new cleaning products and the best ways to use them. These are typical competencies often identified in custodial jobs.

We decided to use a question/answer session and discussion group to assess this competency. After describing the new chemicals and their hazards, we asked the group several questions about the cleaning products. During the session we asked, "You normally work in an adult area, but one day you are asked to clean a public or pediatric area. Would you organize your cart differently that day?"

We had several good answers. One participant said, "I would take all my dangerous chemicals and put them on the top of my cart out of reach of little fingers." Another person said, "I would go one step further than that. I would put all my dangerous chemicals on the top of the cart in a carry-all bucket. When I went on my break, I would take the bucket with me, so none of the dangerous stuff would be left behind unattended."

This is a much more meaningful way to incorporate age-specific aspects into the competency process—one the employees can understand and more easily accept. It is much better than requiring an age-specific competency because "Joint Commission says we have to do it."

Creative Ways To Track and Document Age-Specific, Culture, Safety and Other Competency Aspects.

I believe it is better to integrate age-specific, cultural and safety issues into the competency assessment process rather than creating separate age, cultural and safety competencies. Identify your prioritized competencies first and then add an age twist or a cultural aspect to an already prioritized competency.

The problem with this approach is retrieval of these aspects of competency assessment. If a surveyor asks, "Can you show me your age-specific competency assessment records?" many people wish they had created a separate competency to meet that possible survey request. Don't do it. There is a creative way to track these aspects without creating separate competencies for each of these aspects.

Take the competencies you have already identified and prioritized. Set up a numbering system for each competency. Most educational or training tracking systems can easily be used to create this kind of numbering system. Include in the numbering system a way to identify age-specific, cultural, safety aspects of the work as well as things that may be in response to quality improvement or performance improvement efforts.

Example:

This group identified seven competencies for the time period. They coded each competency with a number representing the year identified, department or work area indicated, and the competency number. After the competency coding number, they added an "A" for age-specific competency aspect, "C" for cultural or diversity aspect, "S" for safety aspect, and "Q" for a response to Quality Improvement monitor results.

Competencies 1, 2, and 6 all have age-specific elements. Competencies 3 and 5 have safety elements. Competency 5 was created because of data collected from a quality improvement monitor. Competency 2 has a cultural aspect in it.

To retrieve this information, all the manager or employee needs to do is ask the computer, "Show me all the work Unit 28 is doing in 2006 related to age." And competencies 1, 2 and 6 should appear.

The manager can also use this same coding system for educational events, in-services, self-learning packets, posters, newsletters, staff meeting topics, quality improvement monitors, etc. Then when the manager asks the computer, "Show me all the work Unit 28 is doing (or has done) in 2006 related to age," the computer will report:

Competencies	Verification Methods	Date Completed
Competency #1 Code: 06-28-01-A	❑ Choice A ❑ Choice B ❑ Choice C	
Competency #2 Code: 06-28-02-AC	❑ Choice A ❑ Choice B	
Competency #3 Code: 06-28-03-S	❑ Choice A ❑ Choice B ❑ Choice C ❑ Choice D	
Competency #4 Code: 06-28-04	❑ Choice A ❑ Choice B	
Competency #5 Code: 06-28-05-QS	❑ Choice A ❑ Choice B ❑ Choice C	
Competency #6 Code: 06-28-06-A	❑ Choice A ❑ Choice B ❑ Choice C ❑ Choice D	
Competency #7 Code: 06-28-07	❑ Choice A ❑ Choice B	

3 competencies (1, 2 and 6)

2 in-services (one on Feb 15 and one on November 5)

1 poster (that is hanging in the medication room on Unit 28, posted on March 22)

2 discussions at staff meetings (Feb 23 and May 15)

1 quality improvement monitor with an age-specific aspect (initiated on Feb 13 currently being done quarterly).

This coding system can help you avoid just a single age-specific competency and instead demonstrate a true integration of age-specific attention into all aspects of your work and outcomes. So you can show not just one competency, but the 9 total age-related activities that reflect competencies, education and outcome measures illustrated above.

Novice to Expert Model

In 1980, Dreyfus and Dreyfus first introduced the idea that in skill acquisition and development there were five levels of proficiency: novice, advanced beginner, competent, proficient, and expert. In 1984, Patricia Benner brought this model to nursing and with it a whole new language to skill acquisition in health care. This has given us a way to discuss and assess a variety of skills needed to be successful in health care. Some organizations have designed clinical ladders and employee recognition programs around this model of novice to expert.

When some people being to look at their competency assessment process, they quickly see a possible link to the novice to expert model—after all, it has the word "competent" right in the middle of it! Some organizations integrate the novice to expert model into their competencies, but then run into confusion because of the way they apply it. Do not use novice to expert levels to judge "where employees are" in a job category.

Example:

If you are assessing IV starting skills using the novice to expert model, you will end up having some novice IV starters and some competent IV starters and some expert IV starters. This becomes confusing for the employees being assessed and for the whole department. What is the true competency expectation for the job category—novice, competent or expert?

Instead, integrate the novice to expert model in each competency. Ask yourself: "What level of skill do we need from this group of employees?"

Example:

In the job category of ICU nurse, you may require that nurses be proficient in defibrillator use. They need to respond to codes throughout the organization. So the minimum expectation is proficient.

In the clinic, you may only expect the nurses to be novice or advanced beginner in defibrillator use. They need to initiate a code and then call for further assistance from the code team. So the minimum expectation is novice.

The novice to expert model can be a great asset to your program. If it is applied appropriately it can help define the level of skill needed for a particular competency. Do not use the model to create a variety of different levels of assessment related to novice to expert. Like any other tool in this book, make sure you understand why you are using it and for what purpose.

Notes

chapter six

Competency Assessment and Performance Review

- Differentiating between competency assessment and performance review

- Defining the overlap between the two processes

- Combining the two processes or keeping them separate

Performance Review

Performance review is also sometimes called performance appraisal, performance evaluation, performance assessment, performance summary, performance rating, annual review, annual evaluation, appraised instrument, etc. (Margrave, et al., 2001). Whatever term you use, performance review is often part of the overall employee evaluation along with competency assessment.

Performance review is a formal management system that provides evaluation of an individual's performance in an organization. It is usually done by the employee's immediate supervisor. The procedure typically requires the supervisor to complete a standardized assessment form that evaluates the employee on several different dimensions and then to discuss the evaluation with the employee (Grote, 2002).

Competency Assessment and Performance Review

Competency assessment and performance review are two separate systems. However, the two systems may sometimes overlap or duplicate efforts. In planning future evaluation efforts, you can choose to combine competency assessment and performance review or to keep them separate. Whichever approach is taken, look for overlap and duplication between the two processes. Take some time to select the appropriate evaluation for each process.

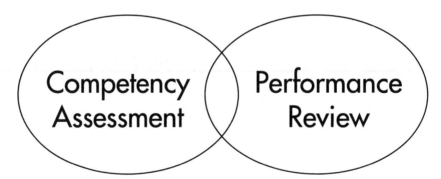

Performance review has a great deal of overlap with competency assessment because of the way it has evolved over time. We often find competencies related to interpersonal and critical thinking aspects of the job in the performance review. This is because our competency programs usually focus on technical skills. Since we have a need to assess critical thinking and interpersonal skills, we often stick them in the performance review. Not because it is the most effective way to assess these skills, but because we know they are important, so we must put them somewhere.

A better approach is to include the domains of critical thinking and interpersonal skills in the competency process, not in performance review. Performance review often relies on the manager's observation and assessment to make judgments concerning these skills. As discussed in earlier chapters, this approach usually is not effective. It is only the subjective opinion of one person—even though it is the boss, it is still just one person's opinion. This is not the best evaluation approach.

The Difference between Competency Assessment and Performance Review

Since competency assessment and performance review are two separate systems, let's look at the differences between the two. While there can be an overlap or duplication in the two processes, each has a unique purpose that is not shared by the other. The unique purpose of each is described below:

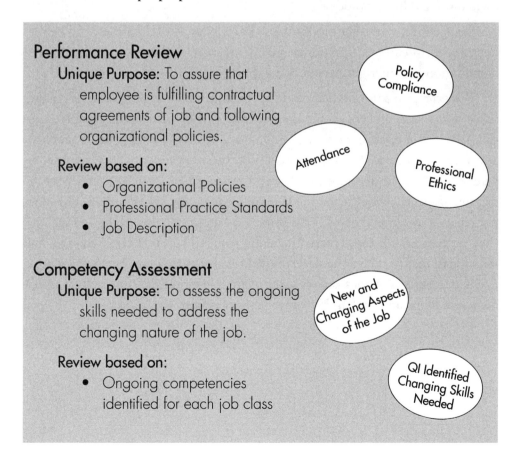

Performance Review
Unique Purpose: To assure that employee is fulfilling contractual agreements of job and following organizational policies.

Review based on:
- Organizational Policies
- Professional Practice Standards
- Job Description

Policy Compliance

Attendance

Professional Ethics

Competency Assessment
Unique Purpose: To assess the ongoing skills needed to address the changing nature of the job.

Review based on:
- Ongoing competencies identified for each job class

New and Changing Aspects of the Job

QI Identified Changing Skills Needed

Competency assessment and performance review share common elements, but also have distinct differences as described in the diagram.

Performance review, although it may cover some of the same territory as competency assessment, has as its main objectives one or more of the following:

- to review the employee's adherence to contractual agreements and organizational policies
- to evaluate the employee's achievement of criteria to keep or advance in a given role
- to determine the amount of compensation appropriate for that effort.

Competency assessment is the process of providing ongoing evaluation of the skills needed to carry out various job functions. Because competency assessment is an ongoing, dynamic process, it will constantly change to meet the demands of the health care environment. Competency assessment should look different in each organization and for each job class in that organization. Although competency assessment shares some characteristics with performance review, it is a different process.

Competency assessment looks at the knowledge, skills, abilities, and behaviors needed to carry out job functions. Its main objective is to make sure the organization has the right person doing the right job.

Competency assessment addresses the dynamic nature of the job. Your competency assessment process should demonstrate this by developing competencies that reflect your organization's quality improvement (QI) efforts, other problematic areas, and new and changing aspects of the environment. This means competencies should be developed each year (or assessment period) to reflect those dynamic aspects. Avoid repeating the same competencies each year. This does not create a dynamic process of assessment. People rarely lose skills and abilities they have acquired; more often the skills required to do the job change, and individuals may not have the skills needed to meet these new demands. By using a dynamic process of competency assessment, you can make competency assessment a more meaningful and effective activity in your organization.

Combining Competency Assessment with Performance Review (or Keeping them Separate—Whatever You Like!)

When considering the design of your competency assessment and performance review systems you have some choices.

You can put them together—having them run on the same cycle with the same deadlines.

Keep them separate—having separate cycles and deadlines for each system, but linking them together by one additional question asked during the performance review process. I will discuss this additional question in more detail in a moment.

Regardless of what option you choose, one thing must be considered in either approach: competency assessment needs to function on a cyclical basis where everyone starts and ends at the same time. Competency assessment does not cycle in alignment with employee anniversary dates. Performance review can be done on anniversary date, but competency assessment *must* be done on a cyclical basis. This is because competency assessment focuses on the job category—articulating the ever-changing nature of that job. It is not focused on the individual, but instead on what skills are needed to currently do the job. Therefore all people in the job category must have the same start and end deadlines. Failing to keep these start and end dates consistent for everyone involved can cause a number of contractual and legal issues.

But what if you want to keep performance review on anniversary dates?

No problem. You can keep performance review on anniversary dates and put competency assessment on an annual cycle, and link the two systems by adding one additional item during the performance review meeting: "Show that you are participating in the competency process."

Example:

Annual Competency Assessment Cycle linked with Performance Review on employee anniversary dates:

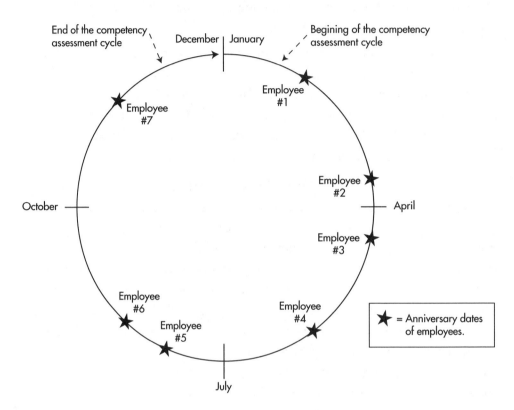

So using the diagram above, during the performance appraisal meeting with Employee #1 (with their anniversary date of February 1) the manager would ask the employee, "Show me evidence that you completed last year's competencies, and do you have a copy of this year's identified competencies?"

For employee #5, whose anniversary date is August 8, the manager would ask the employee, "Did you complete last year's competencies and are you about half way done with this year's list?"

Therefore it does not matter if the competency cycle does not match the performance review date. In performance review we are assessing that the employee is continuing to achieve organizational expectations. This happens, not just at the time of the performance review meeting, but all throughout the year. Not all expectations need to be completed at this meeting time. Managers evaluate every day.

Example:

If an employee arrived late to work one day, we would not wait until the performance review meeting to address this issue. We would address it on the day it occurred.

Subsequently, if someone does not meet the competency deadline (in December as indicated in the figure), action can be taken outside of the performance review meeting time. Performance review is throughout the year; the meeting just happens annually.

Here are some additional examples of other competency cycle options (any of these examples can start on any month of the year to match your budget cycles, fiscals year cycles, or other influential deadlines):

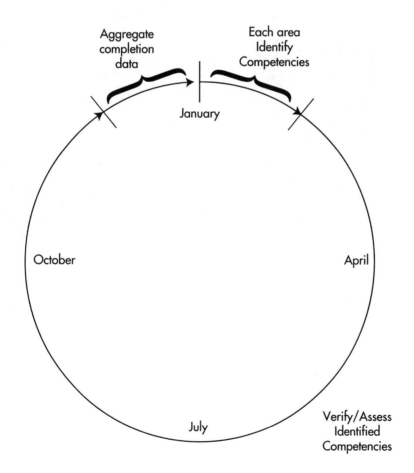

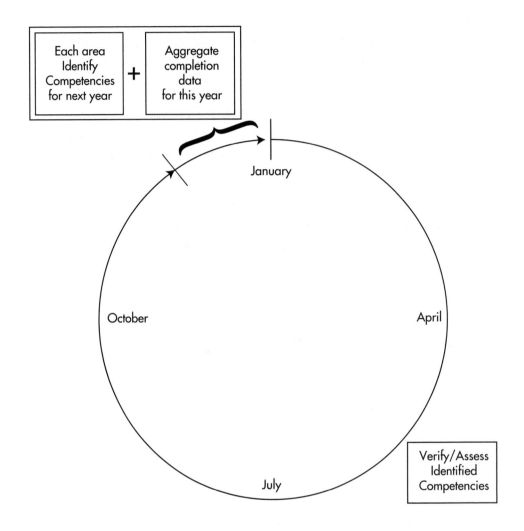

Evaluating Your Overall Employee Evaluation Process

Competency assessment and performance review are just some of the elements organizations use to evaluate an employee. If you examine all the activities of evaluation an organization uses, you will find these activates fall into four basic categories.

By understanding each of these performance evaluation categories, you will be able to make better decision about your evaluation process and how to organize it. You will also have a better understanding of who should be responsible for each of the performance evaluations categories. By having a clearer understanding of these four categories, you can revise any current performance appraisal tool effectively (without the help of expensive consultants who often take old complicated, ineffective tools and substitute them with a new evaluation tool which is just as complicated and ineffective).

One of the most common mistakes in an evaluation tool is trying to evaluate more than one category in a single evaluation item or question. The best and most effective performance evaluation tools categorize items or questions into these four separate evaluation categories. Then the purpose of evaluation is clear to everyone involved in the evaluation process.

Four Elements of the Overall Employee Evaluation Process

Element 1 measures "standards of performance." It reflects the unique purpose of performance review. It reviews the contractual compliance the employee has with the organization. This element is carried out by the supervisor all through the year. If the employee fails to comply with policies and expectations, the supervisor needs to address it at the time. Managers do not wait until the performance review to deal with these issues. Element 1 reflects this process of reviewing compliance and reminds us to document our action plans.

Generally, the part of the evaluation reflecting Element 1 is only filled in if there is a lack of compliance. So it is documented "by exception," which means documentation only occurs if a policy is violated. We would not write down every expectation (or policy) and check off that an individual complied with each during the year. However, some managers start to take this approach—and their performance review forms are getting longer and longer every year.

Element 2 reflects the competency assessment process as described throughout this book. The employee is accountable for verifying his or her identified competencies throughout the year. So this part of the evaluation process will be given to the employee to complete, and then returned to the supervisor at the end of the competency period.

Element 3 provides a way to document any annual requirements of the job. This can include training that is required for that year, required educational events, or current licensure and registration evidence. This section is also carried out by the employee, and the data is brought to the supervisor when completed.

Elements 1, 2 and 3 all come down to a "Yes or No" answer. These first three parts of the evaluation process do not reflect a three-tier response such as "Does not meet, Meets, or Exceeds Expectations." These elements cannot be *exceeded*. For example, these elements do not have a category of "comply with a policy, or REALLY comply with a policy." You can't be competent or REALLY competent. These three sections all reflect an evaluation that comes down to a Yes or No answer.

Element 4 is the one that can reflect the "exceeds expectations" aspects of the job. It is much better to separate this from Elements 1, 2, and 3. This makes it clearer for the employee and the supervisor.

Element 4 can be used to recognize the employee's behavior and performance that exceed the expectations noted in the competencies or performance standards identified. This section can also be used to help create a personal development plan that the employee may want to focus on to achieve their personal career goals and may need the organization's support to achieve. This gives both the employee and the supervisor an opportunity to look at goals for the future, and the efforts needed to achieve those goals.

The Four Elements of Overall Employee Evaluation

1. Standards of Performance   *(filled out by the supervisor)*

This employee has adhered to the contractual expectations of the job as described in the...

- Organizational policies
- Job description
- Performance standards
- Professional practice standards

❑ Yes   ❑ No *(If no, please indicate the action plan below)*

Action Plan:

2. Competency Assessment   *(filled out by the employee throughout the year)*

Competencies	Methods of Verification	Date Completed
Technical Domain		
Critical Thinking Domain		
Interpersonal Domain		

3. Additional job requirements for this year *(filled out by the employee throughout the year)*

- ❑ Licensure/registration current   Exp. Date _____
- ❑ Mantoux test for TB   Tested Date _____

Annual Retraining	Methods of Verification	Date Completed
Infection Control (OSHA)		
Life Support (CPR)		
Chemical Hazards (OSHA)		
Life Safety		

This person has been assessed, and is competent to perform as a

_____ in _____.

❑ Yes ❑ No not yet deemed competent *(If no, please indicate the action plan below)*

Action Plan:

---

4. Recognition   *(filled out by the employee and/or supervisor)*

This section can be used to recognize those employee behaviors and performance that exceeded expectations. This section can also be used to plan a personal development plan that the employee may want to focus on to achieve their personal career goals and may need the organization's support to achieve.

The bottom line of doing performance appraisals is knowing why you are doing them. The purpose is different in every organization. Sometimes the purpose is learning, sometimes the purpose is evaluation and judgment. It is difficult to pursue and accomplish both of these goals with performance appraisal by itself.

Peter Block's observations are noted in *Abolishing Performance Appraisals*, by Tom Coens and Mary Jenkins (Coens and Jenkins, 2002): Performance appraisal is often an instrument of social control. It is an annual discussion where one adult evaluates and judges another. You can soften them all you want to, but if the intent of the appraisal is learning, it will rarely happen in the context of evaluation and judgment.

In many organizations, performance appraisal is little more than a human resources bureaucracy with forms, rules, and review layers. They are often burdens to managers and therefore they are marginally completed (Margrave, et al., 2001)

So as you create, use, and review your evaluation systems, it is important to understand the intent and purpose behind the tool or process. Never use or complete a form or process just for the sake of completing it. We should always know its purpose and *challenge* it if it does not meet our overall goals.

The four elements presented in this chapter will help you organize your evaluation process to clarify its purpose and eliminate subjective and nonproductive evaluation. And let's face it.... much of our evaluation processes are subjective and nonproductive. No matter how many percentages and rating systems you put into an evaluation, it is still often the subjective opinion of one person—your boss. And it is often not productive. We think it will motivate people to perform better. Unfortunately, evaluation often makes people defensive and cynical.

Whatever evaluation system you create, review it with the four elements presented here and make sure you have a system that meets your needs, motivates staff and helps your organization achieve its goals. A thoughtful, effective performance evaluation process, like an efficient, meaningful competency assessment process, can motivate employees throughout your organization.

The competency assessment process shapes the organization. When it is based on accountability and focused on outcomes, it encourages personal accountability and patient/customer focus. We do not assess competency simply to satisfy a set or regulations. We assess competency to create a safe and competent staff—a staff that will give wonderful care and service to patients, residents and our other customers. A truly successful competency process helps us meet our goals of patient safety, excellent service, stunning survey scores, and a healthy work environment.

Appendix

On the following pages are some examples of possible competencies for different job categories. Keep in mind these are not all the competencies for a given job category, just a sample of possible options. The identification of competencies selected for assessment in any job category should be identified by the process shown in chapter 2. Next to each competency statement you will find a few possible verification methods as described in Chapter 4.

Notes

Possible competencies for Office Specialists/Secretaries/Support Staff

Competency Statement	Method of Verification
Task Prioritization/ Time Management: Appropriately and efficiently identifies, prioritizes, and follows through on assignments.	• Peer review/customer review regarding project/assignment feedback • Exemplar of an assignment or project reflecting prioritization and follow through decision making
Phone Triage: Demonstrates the ability to appropriately direct phone calls and requests to meet customers' needs	• Peer review supervisor or colleagues • Customer survey
Room Scheduling: Assigns rooms to meet departmental and interdepartmental needs	• Peer Review • (Quality Improvement) QI monitor to departments regarding room scheduling process and customer service in assigning rooms
Data Entry: Accurate and timely entry of data into computer documentation system	• Evidence of daily work—data is in computer on time • QI monitor of computer documentation
Dealing with People: Applies principals of dealing with difficult people over the phone or in person	• Participants in one of the "Dealing with Difficult People" discussion groups • Exemplar of how the dealt with a difficult situation • Customer surveys
Word Processing: Demonstrates the ability to create memos, letters, and other documents using _____ software	• Evidence of daily work—actual document produced • Teaches/mentors others how to use software package

Possible competencies for Dietary/Food Service Worker

Competency Statement	Method of Verification
Demonstrates the ability to follow a recipe for food preparation	• Return demonstration • Evidence of daily work—daily food preparation
Demonstrates the skill required to handle a customer, patient, or family member who has a complaint	• Case study/role play in the customer service class • Evidence of daily work • Exemplar describing a situation where a complaint was dealt with successfully
Successfully demonstrates safe use of the (new equipment)	• Return demonstration • Evidence of daily work—can operate the device
Demonstrates a basic understanding of food preparation and handling, and the health risks associated with breach on policy	• Completed test on safe food preparation and handling • Video and discussion group exercise on food safety • Presentation to peers on food safety

Possible competencies for Chief Financial Officer & Business Coordinators

Competency Statement	Method of Verification
Creates a fiscal tracking system that provides usable fiscal data to organizational leaders	• Evidence of daily practice (creation of system) • Peer evaluation from leaders involved
Provides expertise and education in reading and interpreting fiscal data	• Evaluation from individuals or groups assisted • Peer review from two other financial coordinators
Demonstrates timely communication of significant fiscal changes to leadership staff	• Peer review from leadership staff • Signature from leadership staff
Demonstrates the use of appropriate fiscal tracking and documentation	• Mock audits of financial records and processes • Actual audits of financial records and processes

Possible competencies for Staff Development Specialists

Competency Statement	Method of Verification
Manages use of educational resources in the most cost effective way	• Completes three cost sheets reflecting proposed education options to respond to educational needs assessment • Presents and explains cost effective strategies at management meeting
Demonstrates role modeling of a healthy environment	• Program evaluations from educational activities • Peer review
Mentors staff in how to create, facilitate and evaluate educational activities	• Peer review • Signature from staff member mentioned
Applies critical thinking to interactions to increase effectiveness as an educator	• Staff or student feedback • Completes an exemplar reflecting critical thinking
Applies the principals of adult learning to educational issues	• Program evaluations from educational activities • Exemplar reflecting adult learning principles application to educational events • Evidence of daily work—objectives, handouts and other teaching material reflects adult learning principles
Supports effectiveness of groups and teams through group facilitation and education	• Peer review from groups assisted • Exemplar reflecting group facilitation
Demonstrates the ability to act as an internal consultant to assist group in assessing a given situation for its true problematic nature	• Submit a completed QI analysis tool used to analyze or diagnose an organizational issue • Consultation evaluation from groups assisted
Demonstrates knowledge of the basic principles of a selected educational or staff development theory	• Attend an educational event or read about a theory and then present what is learned • Exemplar of application of theory into a real life situation

Possible Competencies for Leadership

Competency Statement	Method of Verification
Customer Focus Demonstrates the ability to apply customer service principals to the everyday work situation	• Select two peers/staff to complete the "Customer Service" peer review • Complete the "Customer Service" exemplar
Dealing with Ambiguity Demonstrates the ability to deal with ambiguity, change, and chaos in this dynamic environment of healthcare	• Select two peers/staff to complete the "Dealing with Ambiguity" peer review worksheet
Dealing with Paradox Demonstrates the leadership ability to find the balance in daily situations that represent paradox	• Give a group presentation to peers demonstrating how successfully dealing with a paradox (use the Paradox exemplar form as a guide) • Complete the "Dealing with Paradox" exemplar
Learning on the Fly Demonstrates the ability to "learn on the fly" and make learning a part of daily leadership behaviors.	• Complete the "Complete the "Learning on the Fly" case studies • Complete the "Learning on the Fly" exemplar.
Managing Vision and Purpose Demonstrates the ability to translate the organizational vision and goals into daily actions for you and your team	• Complete the "Managing the Vision" mapping worksheet
Total Quality Improvement Demonstrates active leadership the QI process by carrying out quality improvement activities	• Submit a summary of a current QI project supporting the creation of quality products and services in the organization

Possible competencies for VP of Patient Care Services or Director of Nursing

Competency Statement	Method of Verification
Creates a philosophy of patient care and a model for care delivery	• Submission of actual written documents or policies
Demonstrates the ability to communicate the departmental goals to all managers and staff	• Peer review or evaluation representative of all departments and employees
Demonstrates fiscal accountability for department resources	• Fiscal management data • Exemplar detailing strategies of fiscal accountability
Provides leadership and guidance to other leaders and managers in goal setting, problem solving, resource management, and outcome achievement	• Peer review by leaders and managers
Demonstrates a commitment to a healthy work environment by modeling the desired behaviors and encouraging these in others	• Peer review from any employee with whom there is daily interaction • Signature from any one employee who sees this competency in action
Demonstrates the ability to cope with and manage change, as well as help others do the same	• Self assessment—using the "Coping with Change" self assessment form • Peer assessment—using the "Coping with Change" peer review form
Collaborates with other departments to create systems and problem solve ongoing issues that impact care delivery	• Peer review from peers in other departments • Exemplar outlining collaboration efforts
Incorporates patient satisfaction data and quality improvement data into departmental care delivery goals	• Exemplar describing a plan or goal established with the defined data • Written documentation of goals identified
Demonstrates a clear understanding of regulations applicable to patient care (i.e. Joint Commission standards, State Nursing Practice Act, etc.)	• Evidence of daily practice—(i.e. policy, QI, etc.) created with integration of new regulations • Articulation of understanding though presentation of information

Possible competencies for CEO or Director

Competency Statement	Method of Verification
Creates a vision, philosophy, and mission statement for the organization	• Submission of actual written documents
Demonstrates the ability to communicate the organizational vision, philosophy, mission and/or goals to all levels of employees	• Peer review or evaluation representative of all levels of employees
Provides leadership and guidance to other leaders and managers in goal setting, problem solving, resource management and outcome achievement	• Overall review of strategic planning and other processes • Peer review by leaders and managers
Demonstrates a commitment to a healthy work environment by modeling the desired behaviors and encouraging them in others	• Peer review from any employee with whom there is daily interaction • Signature from any employee who sees this competency in action
Demonstrates the ability to cope with and manage change, as well as help others to do the same	• Self assessment—using the "Coping with Change" self assessment form • Peer assessment—using the "Coping with Change" peer review form
Demonstrates the ability to achieve outcomes within allocated resources	• Fiscal management data • Exemplar detailing strategies of fiscal accountability

Notes

Further Resources

Abruzzese, R. (1996). *Nursing staff development: Strategies for success.* 2nd ed. Philadelphia, PA: Elsevier Science.

Andrew, H., Taylor, E., Davidson, J., Cook, L., and Schurman, D. (1994). *Organizational transformation in health care.* San Francisco: Jossey-Bass Publishers.

Avillion, A. (2001). *Core curriculum for staff development.* 2nd ed. Pensacola, FL: National Nursing Staff Development Organization.

Blanchard, K., Randolph, W., and Carlos, J. (2001). *Empowerment takes more than a minute.* 2nd ed. San Francisco: Berrett-Koehler Publishers.

Bellman G. (2001). *Getting things done when you are not in charge.* 2nd ed. San Francisco: Berrett-Koehler Publishers.

Benner, P., Tanner, C., and Chesla, C. (1996). *Expertise in nursing practice: Caring, clinical judgment, and ethics.* New York, NY: Springer Publishing.

Brookfield, S. (1996). *Understanding and facilitating adult learning: A Comprehensive analysis of principles and effective practices.* San Francisco: Jossey-Bass Publishers.

Connors, R., Smith, T., and Hickman, C. (1994). *The oz principle: Getting results through individual and organizational accountability.* Englewood, NJ: Prentice Hall.

Flynn, W., Langan, P., Jackson, J., Mathis, R. (2004). *Healthcare human resources management.* Mason, OH: Thomson South-Western.

Fournies, F. (1999). *Why employees don't do what they're supposed to do*. New York: Liberty Hall Press/McGraw Hill, Inc.

Fulton, R. (1988). *Common sense supervision*. Berkley, CA: Ten Speed Press.

Gaucher, E. and Coffey, R. (1993). *Total quality in healthcare from theory to practice*. San Francisco: Jossey-Bass Publishers.

Gavin Meisenheimer, C. (ed). (1997). *Improving Quality: A guide to effective programs*. 2nd ed. Boston: Jones & Bartlett.

Goleman, D. (1995). *Emotional Intelligence*. New York, NY: Bantam Books.

Grote, D. (1995). *Discipline without punishment: A proven strategy that turns problem employees into superior performers*. New York, NY: AMACOM— American Management Association.

Gustafson, M. (1996). *The educator's guide to teaching methodologies*. Minneapolis, MN: Creative Health Care Management.

Hakim, C. (1994). *We are all self-employed: The new social contract for working in a changed world*. San Francisco: Berrett-Koehler Publishers.

Howard, R. (ed). (1993). *The learning imperative: Managing people for continuous innovation*. Boston: Harvard Business Review.

Hyland, B. and Yost, M. (1993). *Reflections for managers*. New York: McGraw-Hill.

Jeska, S. and Fischer, K. (1996). *Performance improvement in staff development: The next evolution*. Pensacola, FL: National Nursing Staff Development Organization.

Joint Commission, The, website: www.jointcommission.org.

Kelly-Thomas, K. (1998). *Clinical and nursing staff development: Current competence, future focus*. Philadelphia: Lippincott Williams & Wilkins.

Kissler, G. (1996). *Leading the health care revolution*. Chicago: American College of Healthcare Executives.

Knowles, M., Holton, E., and Swanson, R. (1998). *The definitive classic in adult education and human resource development*. Philadelphia. Elsevier Science.

Kreitzer, M., Wright, D., Hamlin, C., Towey, S., Marko, M., & Disch, J. (1997). Creating a healthy work environment in the midst of organizational change and transition. *Journal of Nursing Administration, 27*(6), 35-41.

Jennison Goonan, K. (1995). *The Juran prescription: clinical quality management*. San Francisco: Jossey-Bass Publishers.

Lang, D. (2000). *Medical staff peer review: Motivation and performance in the eve of managed care* (Rev. ed.). New York: John Wiley & Sons.

Marszalek-Gaucher, E. and Coffey, R. (1990). *Transforming healthcare organizations*. San Francisco: Jossey-Bass Publishers.

McLagan, P. & Nel, C. (1995). *The age of participation: New governance for the workplace and the world*. San Francisco: Berrett-Koehler Publishers.

Miller, M. and Babcock, D. (1996). *Critical thinking applied to nursing*. St. Louis: Mosby.

Morrow, K. (1984). *Preceptorships in nursing staff development*. Rockville, MD: Aspen Publishing.

Nair, K. (1994). *A higher standard of leadership: Lessons from the life of Gandhi*. San Francisco: Berrett-Koehler Publishers.

Nelson, B. (1994). *1001 ways to reward employees*. New York: Workman Publishing.

Owenby, P. (1992). Making case studies come alive. *Training*. January, 1992.

Occupational Safety and Health Administration (OSHA) website: www.osha.gov.

O'Shea, K. (2002). *Staff development nursing secrets*. Philadelphia. Elsevier Science.

Palmer, A., Burns, S. and Bulman, C. (1994). *Reflective practice in nursing: The growth of the professional practitioner*. Oxford, England: Blackwell Science.

Patton, M., Stiesmeyer, J., Teikmanis, M., and Rodriguez, L. (1996). *Manual of staff development*. St. Louis: Mosby.

Robinson, D. and Robinson, J. (1996). *Performance consulting: Moving beyond training*. San Francisco: Berrett-Koehler Publishers.

Schroeder, P. (1994). *Improving quality and performance: Concepts, programs, and techniques*. St. Louis: Mosby.

Tompkins, N., and Machovsky, B. (eds.). (1993). *A manager's guide to OSHA*. Menlo Park, CA: Crisp Learning.

Tracy, J. and Woods, W. (2004). *Competency assessment: A practical guide to the JCAHO standards*. Marblehead, MA: Opus Communications.

Visconti, R., Stiller, R. and Mapson, R. (1994). *Rightful termination: Avoiding litigation.* Menlo Park, CA: Crisp Publications.

Wright, D. (1996). *Creative ways to validate competencies.* Video/Text. Minneapolis, MN: Creative Health Care Management.

Wright, D. (1996). *Tying competency assessment to quality improvement: As easy as riding a bike!* Video. Minneapolis, MN: Creative Health Care Management.

Wright, D. (1996). *How to create accountability through competency assessment.* Video. Minneapolis, MN: Creative Health Care Management.

Wright, D. (1996). *How to create and promote self learning packets.* Video. Minneapolis, MN: Creative Health Care Management.

Zenger, J. (1995). *Not just for CEOs: Sure-fire success secrets for the leader in each of us.* New York: McGraw-Hill Companies.

Bibliography

Benner, P. (1982). Issues in competency based testing. *Nursing Outlook, 30*(5), 303-309.

Benner, P. (2001). *From novice to expert: Excellence and power in clinical nursing practice.* Upper Saddle River, NJ: Prentice Hall.

Coens, T. and Jenkins, M. (2000). *Abolishing performance appraisals.* San Francisco: Berrett-Koehler Publishers

del Bueno, D., Barker, F., and Christmyer, C. (1980). Implementing a competency-based orientation program. *Nurse Educator, 5*(3):16-20.

del Bueno, D., Griffin, L., Burke, S., and Foley, M. (1990). The clinical teacher: A critical link to competence development. *Journal of Nursing Staff Development, 6*(3), 135–138.

Dreyfus, S. and Dreyfus, H. (1980). *A five stage model of the mental activities involved in directed skill acquisition.* Unpublished report supported by the Air force Office of Scientific Research, University of California at Berkley.

Grote, D. (2002). *The performance appraisal question and answer book: A survival guide for managers.* New York: AMACOM—American Management Association.

Joint Commission on Accreditation of Healthcare Organizations. (2004). *Hospital accreditation standards.* Oak Terrace, IL: Author.

Knowles, M. (1980). *The modern practice of adult education: From pedagogy to andragogy.* Chicago: Follet Publishing Company.

Lindeman, E. (1926). *The meaning of adult education.* New York: New Republic

Margrave, A. and Gorden, R. (2001). *The complete idiot's guide to performance appraisals.* Indianapolis, IN: Alpha Books.

Pollock, M.B. (1981). Speaking of competencies. *Health Education.* Jan/Feb 1981.

Reed, J., and Proctor, S. (1993). *Nurse education: A reflective approach.* London: Edward Arnold.

Shaw, D., Schneier, C., Beatty, R. and Baird, L. (1995). *The performance measurement, management, and appraisal source book.* Amherst, MA: Human Resource Development Press.

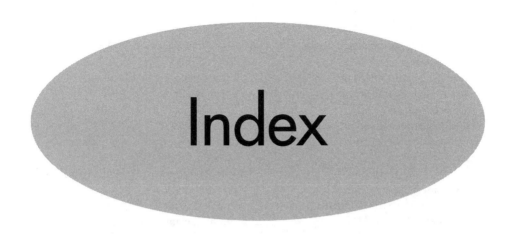

Index

Note to Readers: (frm) designates a form; (fig) designates a figure

About the Author

Donna Wright, RN, MS, is a competency and staff development specialist with Creative Health Care Management in Minneapolis, Minnesota. She received her Masters of Science Degree in Nursing Education from the University of Minnesota. Ms. Wright has helped many health care organizations create meaningful, effective competency and staff development programs for all departments. She has published and lectured across the nation on creative educational strategies, self-directed learning, competency assessment and validation, creative approaches to mandatory training, creating healthy work environments, and implementing shared governance.

Ms. Wright has worked in both staff and leadership roles, and has worked with clinical and nonclinical departments in organizations. Her experiences have taken her to a variety of health care settings, including rural Africa. She is a member and past president of the National Nursing Staff Development Organization and received its "Promoting Excellence in Consultation" award in 1995. Ms. Wright is known for her high energy and refreshing approach to education, competency, and staff development.

Creative Health Care Management provides education and consultation on this topic, as well as many others. If you would like to talk with Donna Wright about competency assessment or need help in creating successful competency assessment in your organization, call Creative Health Care Management at **1.800.728.7766** *or visit* **www.chcm.com.**

Notes

The worksheets listed below have been created to improve your organization's competency program. They may be reproduced for this purpose. You may retype or reformat these worksheets for ease of use if you include the copyright statement at the bottom of the worksheets. Copies of these forms are available from our office.

You may copy and use this page as proof of permission for your files. Please return a copy of this completed form to Creative Health Care Management at:

Creative Health Care Management
5610 Rowland Road, Suite 100
Minneapolis, MN 55343
fax: 952.854.1866
email: resources@chcm.com
800.728.7766

These are intended for your internal use. If you wish to use any of these forms for exhibits, conferences, publication or other external use, please contact Creative Health Care Management.

Creative Health Care Management authorizes User to reproduce the following forms for internal use:

Worksheet for Identifying Ongoing Competencies (page 25–26)

Competency Assessment Form (page 38–39)

Summary of Employee Competency Completion (page 153)

Evaluation of the Overall Competency Process (page 154)

User _____

Department _____

Organization _____

Date _____

Notes

The Ultimate Guide to Preceptoring Video Series

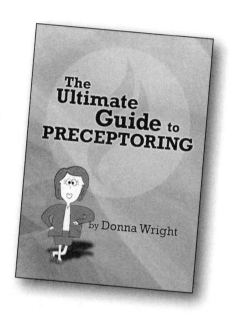

The Ultimate Guide to Preceptoring Video Series provides an entertaining overview of a very practical preceptoring process for health care leaders, educators and mentors. This live 6 session collection plus bonus material shows Donna Wright at her best!

As a whole, these sessions can be used together to view the principles of preceptoring in a wonderful one day workshop or you can view each session independently. Each session has been designed to stand alone so you have the freedom to use this video collection to suit a variety of needs around preceptoring and orientation.

Session Topics Include:

Session 1 - Preceptoring: Orientation and Beyond

Session 2 - Crash Course on Adult Learning

Session 3 - Secrets to TRUE Collaboration (Ms-mS Formula)

Session 4 - Orientation (Parts 1&2)

Session 5 - Partnership: Manager and Preceptor (What Every Manager Needs to Know)

Session 6 - Partnership: Educator and Preceptor

Bonus Session - How Do We Move the OJR (On-the-Job-Retired person) Forward?

We hope you will find this collection informative as well as entertaining! 3 DVDs, approximately 6 hours. (2008)

Notes

Resources for Relationship-Based Care

What   How   What it takes

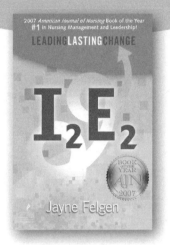

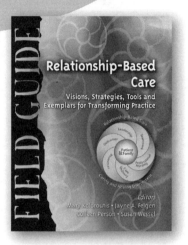

Relationship-Based Care defines the basic principles, presents practical applications and exemplars.

I_2E_2: *Leading Lasting Change* describes the process for initiating and sustaining the necessary cultural change for Relationship-Based Care.

The Relationship-Based Care Field Guide shows how others are implementing Relationship-Based Care across disciplines, departments and organizations.

Our Latest Resource

Notes

The Ultimate Guide to Competency Assessment In Health Care
3rd Edition

1. Call toll-free 800.728.7766 x111 and use your Visa, Mastercard or Discover a company purchase order.

2. Fax your order to: 952.854.1866.

3. Mail your order with pre-payment or company purchase order to:

CREATIVE
HEALTH CARE
MANAGEMENT

Creative Health Care Management
5610 Rowland Road, Suite 100
Minneapolis, MN 55343
Attn: Resources Department

4. Order Online at: www.chcm.com, click Online Store.

Product	Price	Quantity	Subtotal	TOTAL
B1051B—*The Ultimate Guide to Competency Assessment in Health Care*	$34.95			
V310—*The Ultimate Guide to Preceptoring Video Series*	$199.00			
V305PS—*The Moments of Excellence Video Series*	$199.00			
B510—*Relationship-Based Care: A Model for Transforming Practice*	$34.95			
B560—*I₂E₂: Leading Lasting Change*	$24.95			
B600—*Relationship-Based Care Field Guide*	$99.00			
B650—*See Me As A Person (Book)*	$39.95			
Shipping Costs: 1 item = $6.00, 2-9 = $8.00, 10 or more = $10.00 • Call for express rates				
Order TOTAL				

Need more than one copy? We have quantity discounts available.

Quantity Discounts (Books Only)		
10–49 = 10% off	50–99 = 20% off	100 or more = 30% off

Payment Methods: ☐ Credit Card ☐ Check ☐ Purchase Order PO# _____

Credit Card	Number	Expiration	AVS (3 digits)
Visa / Mastercard / Discover	–　　　–　　　–	/	
Cardholder address (if different from below):	Signature:		

Customer Information	
Name:	
Title:	
Company:	
Address:	
City, State, Zip:	
Daytime Phone:	
Email:	